Night Tides

Michael G. Cinquemani

fishtale publications, inc.

Night Tides

The Striper Fishing Legend
of
Billy the Greek

by

Michael G. Cinquemani

fishtale publications, inc.
Long Island, N.Y.

Night Tides

For further information, contact the author at:

fishtale publications, inc.
P.O Box 397
Massapequa, N.Y. 11758
www.fishtalepublications.com

Book design by The Floating Gallery:
331 West 57th Street, #465, New York, NY 10019
(212) 399-1961 www.thefloatinggallery.com

Printed In Canada

Michael G. Cinquemani
Night Tides

1. Author   2. Title

Library of Congress Control Number: 2002095786
ISBN 0-9725501-0-0

Disclaimer

This book is based upon and recounts actual events and experiences drawn from the life of Billy (*The Greek*) Legakis. It is intended to entertain and inform, not to be an instructional guide or "how to" manual. Individuals who elect to pursue activities herein described do so with the express understanding that neither the author nor *Fishtale Publications, Inc.* shall have any liability or responsibility to any person or entity with respect to any loss or damage caused, or alleged to be caused, directly or indirectly by the information contained in this book. Moreover, all readers should check local laws and ordinances as well as federal and state regulations before pursuing any of these activities, which may be governed or restricted by law.

Cover photo: *"The Greek* **heads home hefting his fish and Mike's, who snapped the shot."** (Legakis/Cinquemani) All other photos except as indicated by Billy Legakis.

The photos on pages 85, 122 and 188 appear through the courtesy of **Dick Mermon.** All other photos except as indicated by Billy Legakis.

The author wishes to thank *The Long Island Fisherman* and **Tom Melton**, editor, for permission to use the photographs appearing on pages 34, 122 and 188.

For Rosalie

Who Convinced Me That I Could,
And Helped Every Step Of The Way

"…not so did it seem to Ahab, who knew the sets of all tides and currents; and thereby calculating the driftings of the sperm whale's food; and, also, calling to mind the regular, ascertained seasons for hunting him in particular latitudes; could arrive at reasonable surmises, almost approaching to certainties, concerning the timeliest day to be upon this or that ground in search of his prey."

Moby Dick, Chapter Forty-four, "The Chart"

Prologue

In 1960 a very young Billy Legakis was six years old and lived in southern Florida with his family. His earliest recollections of fishing were of his father taking him to a big local pond to catch large-mouth bass that seemed to him, enormous. Regardless of how many fish they caught, Pete would only take home a single fish for the family to eat, one that was bigger than the metal kitchen sink where it was washed before filleting. These fish were beautiful. Billy was always struck by their huge black eyes that reminded him of the buttons through which his sister's favorite doll saw the world. These fish smelled fresh and sweet. But Billy always remembered one particular fish in that familiar pond. Its size made it unlike any other. Billy, his father, his sisters, would see this fish all the time. They even gave it a name. They hooked it more than once, but never came close to landing it. Four years later the family was to leave Florida for Long Island. Billy walked to the pond alone to get a last look at that big old bass, still surveying her domain, still serene and strong.

And Billy left, never able to understand why it was that that extraordinary fish could never be fooled into being caught.

Records Are Made
to Be Broken

O N A LATE OCTOBER DAY in 1913 a solitary angler by
the name of Charles B. Church dragged an enormous fish weighing just over seventy-three
pounds into his rowboat off *Quick's Hole*, Massachusetts.
That fish was to stand as the world's record striped bass for
nearly sixty years until Bob Rochetta, fishing alone in his
twenty-five foot *Mako* off *Great Eastern* under Montauk
Point bested Mr. Church's achievement by catching a fish that
weighed in excess of seventy-six pounds. Mr. Rochetta's
record, however, was to survive for only two years—for on
the night of September 21, 1982, a stunned thirty-three year
old surfcaster named Al McReynolds was to land a seventy-
eight pound, eight ounce monster on twenty pound test line
off the Vermont Avenue Jetty in Atlantic City, New Jersey.

Since that astounding feat over nineteen years ago, no
heavier striped bass has challenged the world's record status
of Mr. McReynolds' impressive catch.

OF ALL THE species of salt-water fish that claim the northeast coastline of the United States for their home, none has

become an object of greater reverence than *morone sax-atilus*. On Long Island, there would certainly be no argument with this statement. Still, the striped bass does not have the largest following of local fishermen, nor does it have the greatest commercial value. Other local species grow to greater size and many, pound for pound, can test the endurance of a sportsman's tackle more dramatically. Some would argue that other gamefish are more beautiful, others, quicker, others, more aggressive. But no other species evokes the mystique of this extraordinarily handsome silver-gold, black-striped fish. None is more demanding of both accurate and intimate knowledge of the natural environment. None is more directly driven by the wind and the tide, by the currents and the moon-phase—by the infinite and subtle, restless mysteries of the sea. No fish is more challenging to catch. None is more frustrating to pursue. Striped bass, most notably the biggest, solitary members of the species, do whatever they want, whenever they want to. Consequently, few fishermen will sacrifice the countless hours and endless effort that it takes to uncover their secrets and catch them with any degree of consistency. To do so demands taking a giant step beyond mere commitment, into the realm of true obsession. It is a realm that places the quest for striped bass before work, before sleep, before warmth, before food, before comfort, before family, before all.

This book is the story of what would seem to be a pretty ordinary guy living a pretty ordinary life in a small town on the south shore of Long Island. But at the age of twelve, Billy Legakis caught his first striped bass in the breaking waves of a beach near his family's home. It was shortly after that experience that something clicked—or maybe it would be more accurate to say that something snapped—as an element of the extraordinary was thrust into Billy's life. He took the first step toward what was to become his overwhelming passion—and not long afterward, every other consideration in his life was to be relegated to a lower priority than the pursuit of striped bass.

Over the years since his epiphany Billy's efforts have been unrelenting. His achievements, heretofore unchronicled, are so extraordinary in the world of non-commercial fishing that they strain credibility.

Since the early 1970's Billy "The Greek" Legakis has personally landed no fewer than *twenty-five hundred* striped bass in excess of twenty pounds each and every season. Although these numbers may sound like the catches of a professional, Billy is not a commercial fisherman, though he once did fish for the market many years ago. He simply fishes with an intensity and invests a quantity of hours, day and night, that cannot be replicated by anyone tied to the ordinary demands of the normal world. In 1998, the best and most productive year of the past decade for him, Billy landed over *sixty-five hundred* striped bass, including one weighing exactly fifty-eight pounds, four ounces and fifty-seven fish that weighed over forty pounds. In his lifetime, Billy has landed four fish over sixty pounds, with his current best weighing in excess of sixty-four.

The Greek is now forty-seven years old. He has specialized in striped bass fishing for over thirty-five years, the same length of time that has elapsed since I first met him. It is Billy's intention to go to his rest secure in the knowledge that he will be doing so with the world's record striped bass credited to his name.

This book is the story of how Billy Legakis has attempted to accomplish that mission in life.

Everything in these pages is true, although I know that to many readers, especially to most fishermen, some of the stories contained in it will seem to be impossible.

The Chance of A Lifetime

THE SIGHT OF THE FISH STRUCK BILLY. Although still prone to excitement with almost anything possessing fins, *The Greek* was no longer easily impressed. Yet his impulses on seeing this fish were different, because this fish was dramatically different than any he had ever observed before.

Everything else was as it should have been. The darkness of this moonless night was expected. The merging of bay and marsh. The absence of sound. The ironic, distant city-scape twinkling in the face of middle-night—and the bridge lights defining the same geometric margins of the barely rippled bay, below. But this fish was unfamiliar.

This was clearly a bass, an enormous striped bass and Billy of uncanny sight could see the nearly motionless posture of a frighteningly large fish waiting for its meal in the rising tide and the waning hours of the night. All she needed to hold her position in this silent rush of sea was a gentle fanning of her shovel tail and a subtle motion of her gill covers. Every so often Billy could see her turn her huge head, just barely, in primal obedience to ancient instinct. Billy could even see her eyes and the symmetrical pattern of her thumbnail scales. And he could see that unlike any of the other hundreds of fish that he had observed at this same bridge, **this** fish was actually longer than the dark band of shadow cast westward from the structure from which he now peered in disbelief. He could see this fish's head and much of her body, but not her tail.

Billy knew that the band of shadow at this point in the span was five feet wide. This fish, with her nose at the shadow's forward-most edge could not be completely defined by that band—this fish's length had to exceed sixty inches!

Billy did not need to do the calculations. He had caught and released so many fish, so many big fish, so many fifty-pound plus fish that he was stunned by his own mental estimate of what this bass must weigh.

When *The Greek* got excited by big fish, by rare fish, by fish he knew existed but hardly ever encountered, he became even more methodical in technique than his obsession previously demanded. He could not help but become excited—but with Billy, such excitement only heightened his perceptions, made his instincts even more deadly-accurate than they had already been under more ordinary circumstances.

Billy knew, though, he knew that this striped bass could be the fish of a lifetime—and considering the agonizing demands of the *The Greek's* monomania—this was saying a lot. Adrenaline accelerated his heartbeat, but he knew that he had time. Countless hours of experience told him that there was little likelihood that this fish was going anywhere. Even at this pivotal moment in his fishing life he retained enough composure to realize this. The tide had not yet reached its full intensity. Big bass were fiercely territorial and lazy. They earned these rights. They simply positioned themselves in the rush of seawater with a kind of noble arrogance, a seeming indifference reserved for the select few survivors of life's struggle with nature. When and if bait fish struggled by closely enough to the huge head of the cow bass, she would merely flail her gillcovers with sufficient intensity to create a vacuum strong enough to overcome the momentum of her prey. And the great bass would be nourished once again softly, quietly.

THE LINE ON his reel was not old, but not new enough to satisfy Billy who would only leave to chance what he could not absolutely control.

There was time.

He walked more quickly to his van than was his custom. He snatched one of the spare metal spools of fifty pound test monofilament which he always carried as a matter of course. His van, in fact, was actually a highly specialized tackle shop disguised as a mild-mannered, non-commercial truck. No identification. No signage. No vanity plates. No macho leaping fish decals. Nothing. Nothing to even hint at his true mission in life.

But at no time did Billy fool himself. He, more than anyone, understood that monster bass did not get that way by denying their genetically programmed birthright. They were smart, they were controlled—and they were agonizingly selective. He knew that these fish existed, but fully realized that they would not be fooled. Not easily.

Billy's mind snapped back thirty-five years, to the young fishing junkie of a kid lifting the bait locker lid at *Frank's Fishing Station* in Harbor Isle as part of his pre-dawn duties, only to be startled by an enormous striper unlike any he had ever seen, still glistening with sea scent. The magnificent fish awaited shipment to the Fulton Fish Market. He had witnessed lesser treasures of this magical container many times before on many mornings as he struggled to acquire knowledge from the true, secretive masters of Long Island striped bass fishing. Although this bass had been gill-netted it was clearly a local fish—a fish that provided Billy with all the evidence he needed to validate his suspicions. His already respected powers of observation were to be corroborated later that day.

All fish shipped to the Fulton Market in those days were packed and iced in one hundred pound boxes and labeled with the contents, by species. This fish occupied a packing box entirely by itself. The label read:

Contents: *Striped Bass (1)* **Weight: 91 lbs.**

There were not half a dozen men who knew that this fish ever existed. There were not more than a dozen who even suspected that *forties* and *fifties* were being caught with such consistency by a select confraternity of "zipper-mouthed" pin-hookers out of Frank's that they were financing their kids' college educations with them.

But Billy knew, and these distinct memories flooded into his consciousness as he formed a strategy to engage this extraordinary fish.

Escape

EVERYONE KNOWS THAT THE YOUNGER you are the more it is that just a few years seem to separate persons by lifetimes.

I was twenty-two in the late summer of '68, just married, just out of the house, just about to take my first shot at teaching English to hormone-charged adolescents in a corner of southeast Queens.

Billy was fourteen then, gangling and mini-biking. Living in a small house with his family just across the driveway and past a wooden stockade fence, he served as nothing more than an unwelcomed reminder of undefined challenges that lay just weeks ahead with the start of the new school year.

So, apprehensive, I sought diversion at the nearby Long Beach seashore—strolling the boardwalk with Rosalie, flailing the sand with our toes and chasing down incredibly agile sandpipers in the receding carpet of foaming surf.

And in the late afternoon, as we waited for the setting of the sun, fisherman would arrive. They cast and recast their lures between the many stone jetties that crawled seaward every few hundred yards, perpendicular to the beach. Even I knew from their method and the season of the year that their quarry was striped bass, but none ever seemed to actually catch one.

I liked fishing, had for many years, though striped bass remained a deep mystery to me. Now, living practically within the reach of the salt spray drifting north from the breakers of the Atlantic I felt assured that my fishing horizons would expand. Even without a fish though, even without a single fish foolish enough to throw itself onto my unpracticed, naively chosen lure, the rewards of nature would suffice. Of course, a striped bass would be nice. A big striped bass, especially.

In all my weeks of forays into the hidden realm of the striper that followed, however, I had to indeed be satisfied with the majesty of nature, for never was so much as a solitary bass to surrender itself to me.

WHEN I DRAGGED myself home from my first day in the classroom I was mostly numb. I remained that way for quite a while that year, but this is a story about someone else, not a story about me.

Enter Billy, late one fall afternoon, skidding his rear minibike tire to a dust-puffing semi-circular halt before speaking.

In fairness, Billy might not actually have looked as stupid as I first thought, but in those painful days of professional self-doubt I began to mentally reduce the IQ of any young adolescent by a factor of at least two.

"Hey! I seen you leave with a fishing rod a lot in the afternoon, but I never seen you come back with any fish. I'll make you a deal. You drive me over to the beach and I'll show you how to catch a bass—unless you're just another one of those *meatballs* who spends a lot of money on expensive gear and pretty outfits just to watch the sunset."

Great. A wise-ass kid for a neighbor with an arrogance, though evidently not an intelligence, beyond his years. I mentally divided the normal IQ for a fourteen-year-old male by a factor of **four**.

"No, really, it takes me twenty minutes on my bike just to get to the Monroe jetty—plus **you** try riding with a ten foot surf rod and a lure bag. And I got to limit my choices, which really cramps my style. With your car, as pathetic as that thing is—by the way, what the hell **is** that thing 'cause I never saw anything like it before and I know as sure as hell it ain't no Masserati—we can really cover some territory. Really. I can even show a hopeless guy like you how to catch fish. No shit."

This was to be my mentor!
A young teenage Billy in the very early days of *Island Park*.

The car happened to be an Austin *America* and, yes, it was making its model debut in the U.S. that year. Its swan song was to follow very shortly. Immediately, though, I sensed something special about this kid—something more than a good eye for the marketability of cars.

I ALWAYS RATED sarcasm as one of the highest of intellectual capabilities—and sarcasm, the quick, on-the-money kind that honed in and attacked with the precision of today's laser guided ordinance flowed from Billy with unexpected ease. And there was a rough, incongruous facility with words. I was raised on a familial appreciation of verbal sparring, almost always rather cuttingly expressed. The style of this encounter could well have reflected **me** just ten years before. You would have had to be blind not to recognize a promise of something here.

Maybe the gods of irony were forwarding me a compensatory reincarnation of one of the very souls that had begun to frustrate my existence at work each day. So we agreed to meet on Tuesday, right after I got home from work.

"And we'll catch fish too—providing your fine *ve-hi-cle* makes it all the way to Long Beach!"

Late on that appointed afternoon, with the sun already gone, in the pink and orange afterglow of twilight, I caught my very first striped bass. I had been casting a small silver popping plug into the flat water well ahead of the breakers, as close to where Billy, babbling in considerable agitation about frenzied bait and swirling fish, had directed.

The hit was almost instantaneous, though in truth, I had not seen a thing.

Obsession

I N THE WORLD OF FISHING two distinct hemispheres exist. The first represents the world of the familiar and the popular. It encompasses the sportsmen and the sportsmen's tools, the sportsmen's toys and the sportsmen's egos. It is a large and loosely related extended family that embraces technology as the most efficient means to an end. It is the sphere that succumbs to excess in every material aspect of the game, convinced that electronics and hardware will lead to more and bigger catches. It is a confraternity of comparison, of cameras, of substitutes for hard-earned knowledge. Of those who fish, from the most casual to the most "expert," all but the smallest handful operate within the confines of this world.

Then there is the other hemisphere.

It represents the world of solitude, the world of sleepless nights, freezing nights, biting winds, breaking rips. It is the world of silvery bait frantic in the lacy edges of the surf beneath the moon. It is the world of nature still managing to stay one step ahead of science. It is the world of nature herself, hiding her prizes from all those who lack the deep and painfully acquired skills, the commitment, the obsession to delve profoundly enough into her secrets to discover great fish. It is the world of the chosen few. It is the world where Billy, ultimately, was to spend all of his waking hours.

IT WAS AN early Saturday morning in the fall of 1963 when a nine-year-old kid was goofing around with his friends strolling on the beach in the area of Long Beach's "pink" hotel. An old guy, "fifty at least," was out near the tip of a short stone jetty, casting a small metal-lipped swimming plug into the ocean just ahead of him. Even then the boy knew enough about fishing to take note of the outfit—a light one-handed freshwater rod equipped with a *Mitchell* 300 and a blue and white *Creek Chub* lure. On his first cast in Billy's presence the old-timer instantly hooked a fish,which turned out to be unfamiliar to the boy, heretofore accustomed only to small bottom-feeding species. It was a small striped bass. The next cast produced identical results.

Riveted, Billy hopped out onto the jetty, at a respectful distance from the fortunate caster. He could see small spurts of bait breaking all around the tip of the rocks. The third cast astounded him. A huge swirl of water engulfed the tiny plug, the rod doubled over and line screeched off the overwhelmed *Mitchell* reel for what seemed to be only moments before launching seaward with a snapping crack.

Everything but the immediate scene faded into irrelevance, became unreal to Billy.

He heard the vaguely familiar voices of his friends, dreamlike, beckoning in the distance. They didn't matter. He sensed the harsh spray of cold water on his face. He didn't care. He was attuned only to the fisherman and the unseen fish. These things he could feel with an intensity that obliterated everything else. And he knew that the old man knew that he was watching. Billy was stunned when the fisherman turned to him, completely unfazed: "That was a real big one, I had better go home to get my heavier rod."

The fisherman left, but Billy remained. Surveying the scene before him he groped to understand how the elements which he had observed were interrelated. He was already beginning to conclude that the confluence of factors leading to fish could not be simply haphazard.

Wind. Tide. Bait. There was much to learn, much to undertand.

Yet at that moment in time—at that very moment—some yet undefined instinct led him to the decision that this was what he wanted to do.

Although he did not have a clear understanding of how things were to develop from here, this one experience started Billy on the road to what would become his destiny. This moment in time would lead him to a world that nature revealed to only the very smallest society of only the most carefully chosen few.

ONCE YOU ARE drawn into a world of obsession, personal reality can only be found in that world—everything else becomes an exercise in the mundane. For Billy, a world of convention still had to exist, but its significance slipped farther and farther away as the mystical world of the striped bass became more and more real. Every job Billy pursued helped him deepen his understanding of that world. Sometimes, fate even played a hand.

In 1966 Billy was still under the close scrutiny of a

tightly-knit Greek family, especially his keen-eyed mother, Mary. At twelve, he could not easily escape the mandate of New York State's compulsory education law, several well-practiced evasive routines notwithstanding. He was relegated, therefore, to daily pre-dawn beach-front excursions and sunset fish forays, sandwiching school, insignificantly, in the obligatory six and a half hours in between.

In the meantime, Billy's bicycle trips to the beach began to take him across the western side of the Long Beach Bridge on an increasingly regular basis. It was there, from a small parcel of land adjacent to the northwest corner of that span, that John Esposito of the *Commodore Fishing Station* took note of a crazy-looking kid, surf rod held skyward, passing by in the darkness of very early morning, every day, between four and four-thirty. John couldn't help but take a liking to this teenager who showed no sign whatsoever of the universally recognized generational aversion of his kind to the loss of morning sleep. John eventually stopped him and offered him a job.

Billy was soon working for the elder Esposito—readying the station's skiffs, filling outboard gas tanks, packing out bait and helping to rig the party boat, *Commodore,* prior to the customers' arrival at six o'clock each morning. These were mechanical tasks defined by the mundane world of practical need—with one profound difference for Billy. They provided glimpses into another universe. They served as a conduit into the realm of his developing reality.

That's Not Arrogance
Old Man...

MODESTY, EVEN AT THE TENDER AGE of nine, was never one of Billy's strong suits. He never had a problem with self-confidence, and his own personal ramblings have been known to push the limits of credibility at times. Poetic license aside, when Billy speaks of fact, there is always proof to back up the accuracy of his narratives, though many will be tempted to call him a liar, and many have called him much worse.

"I started fishing Long Beach every day, before and after school and sometimes during school if the fishing was real good. I caught a lot of fish. Sometimes it was too easy. Mostly, if you found the bait you found the fish. And I'm not talking about the birds, either. Here's a shocker—birds don't always guarantee fish, and they sure don't guarantee big fish. I'm talking about the bait that you can see in the water— sand eels, mullet, anchovies. Doctors tell me I got better than 20/20 vision today. Can you imagine what it was like back in those days? I really think I see better than most seagulls. I know I see better than anyone else at night. So like I said, mostly it was easy in those days in Long Beach. I was fearless, too. I loved the jetties, no matter how wet or slippery. I watched the sandpipers and learned from them. They never stay too long in any one place. That's what I did on the jetties—you had to bounce from rock to rock. Land too long on any one stone hopping out to the tip of a jetty and you fall on your ass. If you were scared, same thing. It's almost like the rocks can feel you trembling. I loved to watch *meatballs* trying to negotiate their way out onto the rocks. Really, if the fish weren't hitting, they'd take up the slack. It was pitiful, but truly great fun to observe.

All the jetties held fish. The pockets held fish. The surf line between the jetties held fish too, all depending on the tide, the wind and the bait—the bait, most of all. It took me a while to learn these things. If guys on the beach, I mean the really good fisherman like *Lee* and *John* in the sixties, knew you were for real and willing to pay your dues they would teach you amazing stuff. I was a kid, so they didn't have terminal lockjaw with me. I knew how to keep my mouth shut, too. But it wasn't long before I was outfishing all these guys. Smaller fish, mostly, though. A lot of high teens and twenties. We used mainly plugs—*Creek Chub Striper Strikers* were the classic, blue and white, silver, pearl white, which was really deadly. There were plenty of big fish too, but you didn't see all that many. Big fish were in other areas and you'll hear plenty on them later, after I really learned what I was doing.

On the way home I'd usually stop at *Commodore* to pick up a soda and maybe some *Ring Dings*. When John offered me a job, that's when my whole fishing outlook took a serious change. Hanging around that station after closing and in the real wee hours of the morning, I had my eyes seriously opened. I realized that what I had been doing was only playing at striped bass fishing. There was a small group of pin-hookers and commercial guys that the rest of the fishing world didn't even know existed. And sure as hell no one had a clue as to what they were catching. These guys sold their fish, so they would target the money species. They could load up on sea bass, porgies, butterfish—even flounder—but the big bucks in those days was in striped bass, and they went after them with a vengeance. There was nothing fancy about them. They fished from small outboard *Lyman's, Thompson's* and *Grady White's*. They fished the back bays and they fished the ocean from boats—anywhere from the surf line on out. They fished only live and fresh bait—eels, bunker, blackfish—and caught bass that would bring tears to your eyes.

What kind of action am I talking about?

A skiff came into the station at about 10:00 one morning—two guys, one tide—1380 pounds of bass over 40 pounds. You do the math. It happened all the time. And it was going to get even more amazing.

Nobody from the outside knew. These guys were fishing under a blood oath not to talk. Their fish were never photographed, never hoisted up for anyone to see, never bragged about in public, never pictured in fishing columns and they never saw the inside of a tackle shop They were caught in stunning quantities and shipped. End of story.

That was in the late sixties and early seventies. Don't get me wrong, I'm not saying that 'sportsmen' weren't catching fish, everyone knows that those were the glory days of striped bass fishing. I am saying, though, that no one, no one on the outside ever saw fish, size or quantity, like I saw those guys catch day in, day out."

Billy may have said "end of story," but believe me, that was just the beginning.

The stern of *The Greek's* boat in a shot from the early '70's. This was a photo taken **before** the bite really heated up that day!

What it's all about today. Selective fishing for monster striped bass—everything else goes back. This fish was over forty-six pounds.

Photo courtesy *The Long Island Fisherman.*

Days of Wonder

BILLY'S APPETITE FOR INSIDE INFORMATION was exploding. The memory of that first schoolie pulled from the Long Beach surf just a few years before would always remain with him, but his mindset was forever changed. If he had committed to the serious pursuit of bass that morning in '63, he was now approaching a flat-out addiction to the quest for his *holy grail*—finding and catching a world's record fish.

Billy was almost sixteen.

The days at *Commodore* were great days, days filled with revelation, days filled with insight into the deepest mysteries of his growing obsession with striped bass. He knew that the commercial guys didn't see things in quite the same romanticized way, but he was ever grateful that they accepted him into their exclusive society of *cognoscenti,* freely sharing their secrets in exchange for nothing more than hard work and commitment to a vow of silence. It wasn't long, though, before Billy realized that the epicenter of the striped bass scene was located just a few miles southwest of John's station, at the wholesale

The master himself:
Frank Domanick
in 1975.

Thank you, Frank.

The type of fish that
was commonplace
under the tutelage
of Frank.

A very young Billy
with a **40+** fish.

bait dealership of Frank Domanick in Harbor Isle. Frank had heard about Billy and offered him more money to work for him. Given the repository of striped bass expertise reputed to have been secreted away at Frank's, Billy would gladly have worked there for free.

"Frank Domanick's place is where everything really started coming together for me. His wholesale bait operation was one of the biggest on Long Island. We ground up tons of bunker and sorted millions of spearing. Catching bait with Frank probably taught me more about fishing than anything else, because learning about the location, seasons and movement of bait pretty much guarantees that you'll learn how to catch fish. Frank was a great bass fisherman in his own right, but the guys who shipped their fish out of his place to the Fulton Market could all be considered legends of those days. These were the guys who invited me to fish with them, not because they loved me so much, but because I could help them fill their wallets. The truly amazing thing is that there were tons of big fish, forties and fifties, but the market price was highest for the much smaller ones. Big fish were considered almost a pain in the ass—kind of like the way giant bluefins were seen in the old days. Commercial guys would rather haul in teen fish all day. For me, though, the monster fish became my reason for living. And it would be an unusual morning that my eyes didn't pop out as I stared at incredible numbers of beautiful fish—fish to sixty pounds—packed into the storage lockers at Frank's, waiting to be shipped. Really, it happened every day."

MASTER TEACHERS IN any discipline claim to derive their greatest satisfaction from seeing their protegees exceed their own level of expertise. I'm not so sure that the analogy holds up with commercial pin-hookers and gill-netters, but I know that if it did, Billy's mentors would have to be exceedingly pleased. They weren't. Not long after his first few trips with "the boys" Billy started to outfish them.

The guys always had a dollar pool for the first fish, the biggest fish and the most fish. Billy was never permitted a share in the profits—that was the deal—but he almost always managed to collect all the pool money.

Everyone's got an ego. It should come as no surprise that it wasn't long before Billy was on his own. In 1970 he bought his first boat, a used nineteen foot *Thompson.*

The big fish were on the beach, big time. *The Greek* knew where to find them. And, more importantly, he knew how to put them in the boat.

IN TODAY'S WORLD of genetic manipulation it's becoming hard to remember the laws of nature that have been in operation since life forms first crawled out of the ooze. It's becoming even harder to remember that the laws of nature actually work most of the time, providing we don't try too hard to screw things up.

There was a time, centuries ago, when striped bass occurred in such abundance in and around Long Island that they were netted commercially and used for fertilizer when the market price fell too low. There have been times when they've become so rare that it seemed like an entire generation of fishermen might never see a good fish taken in the wild.

Predatory fish are the poster children of the most fundamental dictates of nature's game plan: natural selection and survival of the fittest. Millions of offspring are spawned into the waters of possibility—yet only a fraction's fraction are able to survive the perils of their world even long enough to repeat the cycle. Still, in the natural order of things there is clearly a place for the taking of striped bass by man. The harvesting of striped bass for food and sport by methods respectful of tradition has never been one of the species' greatest threats. Scientifically engineered annihilation and gross ecological insult are other issues.

Yet, for the seeker after truly extraordinary fish there remains a serious moral paradox.

The number of striped bass that survive to exceptional size has never been definitively established by science, yet all experts agree that the percentage must be extremely small. There is no doubt that a great striped bass is truly a fish of great rarity. It would not be difficult to conclude that the taking of these noble creatures was tantamount to driving the species into extinction and that the successful hunter after these enormous fish must be one depraved and totally callous to the laws of nature. But just the opposite is true.

The older theories that the very biggest fish are the most prolific has been proven wrong through direct, anecdotal observation in hundreds of cases. A lot depends upon the definition of a big fish. Billy is convinced that the main spawning stock consists of fish in the thirty-six to forty-five inch (i.e. low twenty to forty pound) range. These are the females that are consistently loaded with roe during the spawning season.

"It is extremely rare to find viable roe in fifty-pound plus fish—and I've never personally caught anything over fifty-eight pounds with live roe. I've personally caught over a hundred fish over fifty pounds and I've observed many hundreds that were caught commercially in that category. Not ten percent of all these fish contain living roe, which is pinkish to orange in color as opposed to the brownish-green of dead roe. And no fish carrying roe into the deep summer when the water temperature is too high can produce a viable spawn, anyway. As sad as it may sound, these real big fish are in the final stages of their life cycle. Every season I live by a strict personal policy of keeping only progressively larger fish. If I get an early season fish of forty-five pounds, I will only consider keeping a fish that beats it. I say 'consider' because I no longer keep fish that are not extraordinary, or an occasional one requested for food. I don't gaff fish or net them, no matter what the size. I don't touch a fish's gills or even take them out of the water if I'm not going to keep them. I never gut-hook fish because I never let fish run for more than two seconds, regardless of the bait. I consider myself a conservationist today. At any rate, when I keep a really beautiful fish—a fish over fifty pounds—I'm convinced that I'm not hurting the breeding stock, because I've never observed a female bass of this size that is still capable of breeding."

Today, modern fish biology seems to be coming into agreement with Billy's long held observations.

In the impetuosity and ignorance of youth, Billy equated quantity and kill rate with success. There was no shame in loading the boat with eighteen hundred pounds of teen-sized fish when they helped pay to support your family, or, less nobly, when they helped prove your worth to an unreceptive cadre of disbelievers. But the days of incredulity were not to last, and it was not long before *The Greek* had nothing to prove to anyone other than himself.

But these were still the golden days of easy success.

Billy's oath to himself could not be fulfilled until the cycle of nature once again took its downward turn, secreting from discovery the pods of great fish that would make themselves known to only a tiny group of extraordinarily skilled fishermen who had themselves become as rare as the very fish they sought to encounter.

But in the early seventies there seemed to be no end to the numbers of great striped bass. They frequented their haunts with the consistency of moths to a flame on a warm summer evening.

Days of Madness

WHEN SPEAKING OF FISHING, it's always hard to avoid exaggeration—positive or negative. This is especially true when a good part of the game has to do with concealing or distorting information. When a resource is limited and valuable, be it gold nuggets or striped bass, sharing accurate information with the competition is just plain stupid. But the ego is a wonderfully powerful force and few among us can pass up the opportunity to seize a moment of glory.

While serious fishermen are more tight-lipped than a team of archaeologists guarding the secret to the entrance to Amon-Ra's tomb, the average weekend warrior can't resist the urge to hoist a hefty cow in front of a camera, complete with a blow by blow description of time, tide, bait and location. A psychological dilemma should be clear. You either keep the address of the mother lode hidden for as long as possible, or you revel in your moment in the sun—along with the onslaught of every new kid in town hell bent on similar fame and fortune.

Human nature being what it is, by the early seventies the word was out and it was only a true *meatball* who never caught on that the fruit was ripe for the picking.

During those days, bluefish was king on the south shore of Long Island. There were no bag limits and the dozens of party boats that sailed from Sheepshead Bay to Montauk Point bunker-chummed enough fish, day and night, to satisfy the most voracious sportsman. Virtually anyone could catch his fill of blues. Striped bass, on the other hand, still enjoyed an elitist aura, and they retained their reputation as a fish that could only be caught consistently by expert fishermen.

Legends like Frank Domanic and his cronies had closely guarded the art of chumming with clam bellies in the late fifties, but it wasn't long before everyone had caught on. The commercial guys had no intention of tipping their hand and went so far as not to fish at all if they had any kind of an audience. This was commonplace (and fully understandable) for fishermen who had to protect their livelihood. But in the mid-sixties a small cadre of highly secretive fanatics began utilizing a technique for catching giant striped bass that was so deadly its revelation would temporarily alter the long-standing reputation of this great fish as one which separated the men from the boys. Needless to say, the secret was not to be guarded very long. Soon, anyone who could run a skiff out of a south shore inlet and locate a school of bunker was all but guaranteed cow bass at a ratio of one fish per live bait swum out near the tip of virtually any jetty. Rank amateurs began to talk about how it was harder to catch bunker and keep them alive than it was to catch bass. So the bunker were used dead. And they caught bass, too, often even better than their live and kicking counterparts. *Long Beach*, *Lido*, *Atlantic Beach*, the *Rockaways*, *Breezy Point*, the *Jersey Highlands*—it didn't matter a whole lot. Find the bunker and you found the fish. If you couldn't find the bunker, you'd find a bunker boat and buy a dozen "pieces" for close to nothing. Next thing you know, "Bam!" An instant generation of sharpshooters was born. Eventually, bait and tackle shops caught on and you could purchase "fresh dead" bunker from the comfort of your local retailer's establishment and enjoy the camaraderie of all the new "expert" striped bass fishermen to boot.

"I mean, it was really crazy. I was thirteen or fourteen when this whole thing broke loose and I was routinely catching eight to ten fish a day, all between forty and fifty pounds. There was no limit on fish, except that they had to be over sixteen inches. If you could sink your boat with forties and fifties, that was OK. The *Sheepshead Bay* boys never did less than six hundred pounds a day, usually more like twelve hundred pounds. *Six hundred pounds* of forty pound plus fish was considered a bad day. Every *meatball* came back with the fish of his lifetime and wasted no time running it over for an official weigh-in at a local tackle shop. Back then, everyone was a hero, although I doubt that anyone would use that word today. All the local fishing magazines ran pictures of guys surrounded by circles of forty pounders. I know they wouldn't do that today, even if it was legal and anyone could ever repeat those catches. Tackle shop bulletin boards covered over shots of guys with forty pound fish with *Polaroids* of guys with fifty pounders. It was insanity, it was madness, it was the California Gold Rush, only with striped bass, and we all know how long that lasted.

Looking back, I don't think that anyone was really proud of what we did and how easy it was to annihilate fish in those days. I'm probably the only guy who can still put up quality and quantity like that, but I'll never kill fish that way anymore. It was a feeding frenzy and everyone got caught up in the scene. We'll never see days like that again, at least not in my lifetime."

But *The Twilight of the Gods* was rapidly approaching.

It's hard to say what combination of factors—environmental, ecological, or regulatory—led to the bursting of the bubble, but the impact of years of absurdly easy fishing could not have helped matters. Billy is known for his ability to think like a striped bass, a talent which he has always considered prerequisite to success, but he also allows for the turning of the tables in crediting striped bass with the ability to think like him. He therefore submits one additional factor for the collapse of bunker-dunking as the turn of the seventies' decade approached: *the bass's ability to learn.* Whether by instinct of nature or by a more highly developed, anthropomorphisized intellectual facility, Billy has always been convinced that the wise old cows in residence off the beaches of the south shore eventually caught on to the drill being practiced by their pursuers. Lost fish somehow "communicated" the set up to their brethren, making the experienced older fish far more wary of oddly swimming mossbunker—and the rapidly growing number of bunker being presented through a no-longer-innovative fishing method made what had previously been fierce competition for a select group of vulnerable targets far less aggressive.

But Billy continued to accept and live by one fundamental reality:

"Big bass are excruciatingly selective feeders. They don't have to eat very often and will rarely go out of their way to actively pursue a meal. When a feeding opportunity makes itself available, a wary old bass rarely has more than a split second to make its decision to eat or not to eat. You can only be successful with hooking large striped bass if you effectively take advantage of the fish's natural and powerful instinct to nourish itself when opportunity arises. You must recognize and accept, however, that the instinct of nature is not entirely overwhelming. A mature fish possesses the ability to subjugate its potent urge to feed opportunistically to its even more extraordinary capability to pass up a meal, even when close to starvation, when she senses danger in the form of anything unnatural. She must make the decision to feed instantaneously—and will almost always allow a perceived meal to escape rather than risk danger or death, which to her are one in the same. That is why she will endure young fish that engage in a feeding frenzy yet never, sulking in the depths below, let her presence be known. That is why she will allow a bucktail with no more than a single hair out of place to drift harmlessly past her nose without exerting so much as the minutest effort to suck it into her cavernous mouth. That is why she will eventually learn to ignore the siren call of the tantalizingly fragrant offering struggling so enticingly just beyond the flip of her powerful tail. That is why she sometimes, some very rare times, survives long enough to attain staggering proportions."

That, along with the insult done to these noble fish who swam in such great numbers just beyond the southern reach of the breaking waves along our beaches, is one of the most significant reasons why the unbridled attack upon the great striped bass came to such an abrupt end in the opening years of the decade that was to follow.

EVENTUALLY, BILLY'S SENSE of conservation was to evolve from a combination of a love for fish and an almost devilish disdain for anyone unworthy to kill a bass. You were "unworthy" in Billy's eyes if you possessed nothing more than dumb luck and stumbled into a fish, especially a good fish, with little or no expertise.

Big striped bass epitomized the amazing ability of any animal resilient enough to survive to old age in a hostile environment by struggling against the challenge of the elements, by developing an extraordinary sense of caution, by exhibiting stunning restraint against the primal, instinctive calls of hunger. Such an animal became independent. Such an animal became wise.

To be worthy of taking such a fish's life you had to understand these things on a level so elemental that you literally thought like the fish, understood its life's struggle and empathized with its fate.

Small fish didn't count. Small fish were impetuous adolescents lacking the maturity, the simple sense, not to leap into oblivion after any gleaming trinket. Any fool could catch small fish. Small fish were hell bent on suicide. Small fish didn't count.

So in the midst of any blitz that somehow centered only around the magical waters circumscribed by Billy's aura (in the rare instances that he could be **witnessed** taking fish after fish while others beat the barren waters) he would often hoist a good bass in plain sight—only to release it with conspicuous ceremony that would invariably leave onlookers muttering and cursing in frustration. I've heard many a slickly-outfitted surfcaster on the verge of doing serious harm, golfer-like, to his prized equipment, swallow his "pride" and actually ask Billy for a fish that was about to regain its freedom. Billy's signature response rarely varied "Sure, this one's pretty stupid, catch him!" And so, another beautiful bass would slide off to freedom through the foaming surf.

Kids, struggling neophytes, old men and the clearly ill-prepared, however, were different. United by the common traits of sincerity, humility and a real desire to learn, they would often receive invaluable, even secret information and advice from the master.

But let's not carry the perception of philanthropy too far. This could occur only when Billy wasn't drawn away, elsewhere, suddenly, by the proliferating demands of his obsession.

The Only Thing
That Stays Is Change

I T WAS THE MARKET CRASH OF '29 and the fallout of
Greenspan's "irrational exuberance" speech rolled into
one. The days of the overnight hot shot were history
and only the true die-hards willing to pay their dues the old-
fashioned way were going to survive. Snapshots of beautiful
bass either yellowed with age on tackle shop bulletin boards
or got covered up with glossies of the returning weakfish, or
tuna or even fluke. The government stepped in, year class
statistics got dissected, and the striped bass was declared off
limits to all recreational and commercial fishermen. The epi-
logue of the east end haul-seine fishery was being written.
People shook their heads and marveled at the awesome ability of nature to turn feast into famine. And Billy reveled in
the isolated glow of opportunity.

When the going gets tough in the fishing world, one of
two things generally takes place: you either use the adverse
conditions to justify why your focus has changed to another
species that is available in greater abundance, or you thank
God that the masses have relinquished their previous quest to
the few remaining fanatics. In the early eighties, though,

even the most serious bass fishermen were licking their wounds. A total moratorium on all bass fishing had been declared and it would be several years before any momentum would be restored to the fishery. Only a handful of true believers even considered the hunt any longer worthwhile.

Theories abounded as to what happened and how the striped bass would never return. The *EPA* had a convenient argument to justify the restrictions that were imposed on the commercial boys and the public at large was impressed with the government's oversight of their food supply. Even the unscientific among us knew that *PCB's* would make you glow in the dark some day if you ate too much bass or even bluefish (thank God at least the tuna supply was now miraculously consisered safe). If nature did not repeatedly demonstrate her amazing resilience, the pursuit of these theories might be of some interest—but the fact is that the striped bass had not disappeared from the face of the earth—they had not even disappeared from the western south shore of Long Island. They were there, but circumstances had changed and extraordinary skills would be required to locate and catch them.

"True, there are fewer fish and smarter fish today, but there are still plenty of bass and many are giants. Most guys think the big fish are all gone. Bullshit. The only thing that's gone are the guys who know how to catch them. Just check out the pictures in this book, along with the dates they've been caught—and remember that I don't keep more than a fraction of what I actually catch. You tell me that the big fish are all gone after checking out my numbers."

The bad news for the masses is that there are no real short cuts or secrets to catching big striped bass today. The closest thing to a guarantee would be to have an exceptionally skilled sharpshooter show you exactly what to do under a given set of circumstances. Other than with a professional guide, though, that arrangement would be oxymoronic. Sharpshooters stay sharp by guarding their secrets and misleading the competition. Billy has hooked fish after fish on bucktails, right alongside of me, as I, copying his every move, have gone hitless for the trip. This is not to say that skills cannot be learned, only that it takes time and commitment.

"In the early days—the fifties and sixties—there was no such thing as 'how to' manuals. Almost no one knew the real productive techniques. Would you believe that only the pros actually fished at night? All the secrets were kept between us. It took twenty years before anyone on the outside even figured out that big bass ate flounder! Periods of abundance always create a shitload of experts. Only when the fish get smart do you find out who the real fishermen are. Then all the former 'experts' go back to bluefishing."

The 1980's—The so-called "decade of no big fish."
The Greek still had them.

The family gets in on the act.

At What Point Do You
Call It Insanity?

O N THE SECOND NIGHT AFTER HURRICANE Gloria most of the electricity on the western south shore of Long Island was still out. I'm sure that most of the rest of Long Island was also incapacitated, but I knew my own neighborhood first hand. Nothing in my all-electric household worked and the scene up and down Merrick Road was one of eerie darkness. Reports started trickling in that the *Nautilus Diner*, just two miles to the east, had its own generator and was functioning normally. The lure of cheeseburger deluxe platters proved too much to resist and within an hour my wife and I were slathering ketchup on our fries.

I had not seen Billy nor his wife Dee in years, but the raspy tone of an unmistakable "Is that you, *meatball?*" combined with the sight of a uniquely mustached countenance told me that I was once again in the presence of *The Greek*. We exchanged the ordinary updates of friends who had not seen each other in years before Billy's talk turned to the intensity of the weather and his feeling that the bass might be in a feeding mood as a result. He asked if I wanted to join him to check out the action. I stared over at Dee with the obvious question in my eyes.

"Oh, yeah, Mike—he's serious—and he'll supply you with the live eels he had to transfer to my bathtub because of the blackout, too."

Trees down, winds still up, waters still churning a maelstrom of froth—and Billy wants to go bass fishing—with the live eels he now had in his bathtub! May I drop my yet unseen forty pounder at the boat if I'm exaggerating or bending the truth.

Now, how do **you** spell obsession?

I didn't go that night, but I did start to get together with Billy on the occasions when he had the patience to drag me along on some of his less-secretive expeditions. Mind you, I never really got the impression that I was being guided through the darkest convolutions of Billy's fish brain, but I did catch bigger fish, and more of them, than I ever thought existed.

Although *The Greek* saw life strictly in terms of striped bass, all his time on the water couldn't help but turn him into an expert on other species—collateral victims of his monomania. I had owned a boat in the early seventies, the heyday of the weakfish's resurgence in Great South Bay. Unlike my obsessive sometimes fishing buddy, I was elated to hook anything. I became an expert at catching all kinds of impetuous, stupid or otherwise desperate fish. Five to seven pound weakfish were committing suicide on the infamous pink Bagley's *Salty Dog* all along the edges of western Fire Island. As one yellowfin was reeled to the waiting net, several of his brethren would follow him to the surface, anxious next victims. You can bet I was part of that mosquito fleet on a regular basis during each of the years before the action petered out. When small fluke started to repave the bottom of Reynolds Channel, the inlets and surrounding bays, I was there, squid and killies in tow. When mackerel schooled in packs so tight that diamond jigs would bounce off their bodies on the way down, I would even venture an offshore trip, lured by the guarantee of action.

Now this was my kind of fishing, but it wasn't Billy's.

By the mid-eighties the cycle of *cynoscion regalis* had once again fallen sadly into oblivion and the secretive process of rejuvenation was left in nature's hands. I bemoaned the virtual disappearance of a great fish that had made me an "expert."

THE PHONE RINGS. Midnight. It's reacquainted "hurricane" Bill asking if I'd like to catch some humongous weakfish with him.

"But Billy, the weakfish are all gone, even I know that—you must have awaken from a dream about them—and two a.m. is not my favorite fishing hour, anyway." But I'm still enough of a fisherman to be intrigued by the next part.

"Mike, I'm telling you that if you want to catch teen-size tiderunner weakfish tonight, get your ass out of bed and I'll pick you up in half an hour. We have to be at the spot by two."

"What do I bring? How are we fishing? Where are we fishing? What are we fishing with?"

"I'll handle all of that. That's why *meatballs* and 'museum pieces' like you never catch fish. Do you want to go or not?"

I had heard that weakfish could get really big—and had read about fish up to the high teens in the last years of this fabulous run—but I had never actually seen one. True, it was common knowledge that weakfish in our area were history, but how could I resist?

By 12:45 a long maroon van was idling outside my front door. We sped off into the darkness, south down *Wantagh Parkway*, west along *Ocean Drive*, north across the big *Meadowbrook* span—assisted by a few slick moves that would have caught the immediate attention of the guardians of our state highways in less somnolent hours.

I was soon to learn that our objective was actually the span of the bridge, itself. Billy positioned his van to effectively obscure the "NO PARKING AT ANY TIME" sign that loomed conspicuously as we pulled up to the chosen location. *Greek* broke out several outfits, all conventional, all heavier than I had been accustomed to. No lures of any kind appeared to be rigged. I was puzzled. Billy stalked the western walkway of the bridge, south to north and back again staring into the illuminated arches of light and the darkness of the water. The tide was running out. Small white splashes of something punctuated the blackness. It was so quiet that you could hear the disturbance as well. We were all alone.

Even at that late hour during what I knew to be a normal workweek, however, an occasional car shot frighteningly by. I cursed, but Billy didn't even seem to notice. How could he? He was fixated on the small white splashes below which he joyously concluded were produced by the resident bunker—which he advised were prerequisite to our success that night and therefore a promise of great things to come.

Billy was the professor. I was the student. All I had to do was watch and learn.

The Greek flipped a weighted treble snagging-hook into the running tide. A few sweeps and jerks of the rod later and a fat bunker was soon impaled and swimming enticingly below. Meanwhile, I utilized Billy's twin backup rig. Sweep, jerk...nothing. Sweep, jerk...nothing. Why the hell bother to use conventional tackle, anyway? Billy mercifully relieved me of my rig, now in the throes of its third bird's nest and handed me the rod with the thumping bunker attached. I was still baffled. Where were the pink *Salty Dogs*? What were we doing with bunker anyway, going bluefishing at sunrise?

Billy did not fish, concerned more with the immediate success of the incredulous *meatball* who had the audacity to question his methods and expertise. Instead, he continued to expertly snag all the bait we needed. I was told that the fish would not hit very hard but that the bait would be "picked up" and had to be fed to the fish.

"What fish, Billy? What weakfish is even big enough to get this bunker-on-steroids into its mouth?"

Within minutes, I was to find out.

I was actually enjoying the tug of the swimming baitfish at the end of my line. I was thinking that they were pretty strong fish. Imagine a ten pound bunker!

If a picture is worth a thousand words, an actual "pick-up" is worth a thousand pictures. Billy had told me to count to ten, and amazingly, I took his advice. When I flipped the reel into gear and leaned back, I was shocked to feel powerful resistance. It was many years ago, and I can't remember all the details, but I can tell you that "we" landed the fourteen and a half pound weakfish that I hooked shortly after our arrival at the bridge that night. I proceeded to hook and land (Billy has a method all his own, which I'll eventually get to) five fish that night going to over sixteen pounds. I still have the pictures to prove it. Billy caught nothing himself, only because he wanted to prove a point to me.

He did.

As the sun came up at our backs that morning some unknown fishermen approached the bridge on foot to begin their day. They appeared from nowhere and did not seem to have a car. By that time, however, all forms of the night's fish activity had disappeared to points unknown, precisely as Billy had predicted. There was no longer any indication of bait nor any indication of fish. *The Greek* had already secreted our tiderunners away into the cavern of his fish box in the back of the truck. I was amazed to see that the cooler had already been half filled with the fruits of Billy's earlier exploratory labors. I could not resist the opportunity to "accidentally" display my sixteen pounder in full view of the newcomers in order to revel in the glory of "my" achievement.

These guys were Hispanic. I knew their native tongue well enough to pick up an animated exchange combining elements of amazement, incredulity, curses and the general misuse of the Lord's name.

Needless to say, Billy was pissed.

But how could he stay mad at a *meatball* like me?

THE WEAKFISH EVENTUALLY did leave. That was expected. Old-timers had always talked about the dramatic cyclical nature of the species. But far more ominous was the talk that started to circulate in regard to striped bass—talk of the end of the species on Long Island—even talk of possible extinction.

The *DEC* stepped in and the rest was pretty much history: no recreational fishing for bass, a total ban on the commercial fishery for four years, and dramatic curbs on the taking of fish by both groups in the foreseeable future.

"I can't argue with the steps the DEC took because they didn't really have a choice. I mean the combination of factors working against the fish was deadly. Anyone bothering to pay attention knew for a long time that something drastic had to be done. There were all kinds of theories for the bass disaster, but I see it like this. First (maybe not scientifically first, but this was a major factor to me) big bass had become such suckers for easy fishing methods that the main body of breeding fish was being wiped out, not just on the Island, but everywhere along the striper coast. Everyone knew that big time environmental issues and pollution in the Hudson, the Chesapeake, and the other critical breeding grounds were contributing to the death of the fishery. Then there was the normal cycle of nature—the *feast or famine* phenomenon. It all came together to kill the fishing. It was no surprise. Plenty of us had seen it coming for years. The truth is a lot of pretty sharp people figured it was already too late.

Naturally, the complete striped bass moratorium—followed by real tough minimum size limits on later catches pissed off everyone in the world—except for the conservationists, of course. Haul-seiners out east witnessed the end of centuries of tradition, charter boat captains all over watched big bucks evaporate from their operations, bait and tackle shops got some of the wind knocked out of their sails —and recreational fishermen cried a lot. I'm not sure about these last guys, though, because most of them couldn't catch a bass when the going got tough anyway."

But give nature a chance to take its course and amazing things sometimes happen.

In just a few years *roccus* managed to bounce back with considerable vengeance. It wasn't long before even party boat captains were getting in on the action. And the timing couldn't be better. Adding sailing schedules for a glamorous species like striped bass helped to bring back customers, many of whom were starting to become disenchanted with bag and size limits on blues, weakfish and fluke.

Yes, the hunt was definitely on once again—though for a guy like Billy, I knew it had never really been off.

Dee Legakis. She only likes catching the smaller stripers.

The man himself. Billy in a rare photo without a bass.

"Night Tides; very big striped bass."

THE GREEK HAS pursued every possible method for catching striped bass, each with equal fervor. He knows no other way. But for the most concentrated learning experience, for gut level insight into the way big bass actually think and react—he has always favored fishing the bridges. Most fishermen think of "bridge fishing" as structure fishing from a boat, drifting clam bellies into the pilings or dragging eels around the abutments. Billy does that too, but to him "bridge fishing" really means fishing from the **top** of the structure.

"Everything—I mean **everything** from the top of the bridge is visual. If you want a real intense education in catching big bass, spend your time studying the scene from the top of a well-lit bridge. Evcry single factor that is part of the bass equation comes into play—location, structure, tide, bait, wind and presentation—especially presentation. It's all there like you're seeing it on videotape, providing you have the eyes to really see, plus a whole lot of time and a whole lot of patience. And providing you don't love sleeping late at night.

When all the conditions are right, though, there is nothing that can match the scene spread out in front of you in the shadowline of the right bridge. There will be times (and don't get too excited, because this isn't going to happen a whole lot) when the biggest bass you have ever dreamed about will line up like logs in the current. These are the monsters that have followed the biggest baitfish into the bay. They're the *late cruisers* that will be the last to leave as the water temperature drops. They are ruled by nature's compulsion to feed intensely in preparation for their marathon swim to points unknown—but they will never expend unnecessary energy in doing so. They won't chase bait—you'd think that they would, considering their tremendous strength and hunter instinct, but trust me, they won't. They will always wait for the current to bring food to **them**. I have watched these fish over and over again ignore everything, and I mean everything—including natural forage, live baits that looked good enough for **me** to eat—and lures presented with the precision of a brain surgeon. They didn't get to this point in their lives by being careless. But when the planets line up and the gods smile at you—when your bucktail is picked up by the current at the precise spot that combines with the influence of the wind and tide on your line—when your lure drifts past the nose of a monster at the exact right speed and the perfect depth—then her pectoral fins will start to vibrate (you can actually see this) and you will know that she has made the irrevocable decision to inhale your offering. This only happens at bridges, and you see it all right in front of you. That's if you're really good, **and** really lucky. Most of the time, these giant fish will just keep you talking to yourself. If you can't handle this scene, stick to something else. You may never catch a monster, but it'll be a lot better for what may be left of your mental stability. Trust me on that."

Dreams Under A New Moon
In November

A very dark night in the very late fall of 1978.

I T HAD BEEN A GOOD YEAR for almost everyone, but
thoughts now turned away from fishing and toward the
frigid hiatus imposed by winter. Earthbound gulls in
Parking Field Six huddled together, their backs to a foaming
gray ocean; they pressed their feathered white underbellies
to the dark asphalt of the empty lot, absorbing the last ves-
tiges of autumn's residual warmth.

A strong wind was blowing from the northwest. The tide
raced in from the sea, accelerated by the constrictions of
Jones Inlet. The bridge was deserted. There was no longer
any reason for cars to be rushing by, and none disturbed the
stillness of this night. A lone figure surveyed the water from
atop the southwest corner of the desolate structure. He, and
perhaps only he, still expected signs of life in the flowing
chiaroscuro below him. He was not disappointed. Late
arriving herring were clearly visible struggling against the

powerful current in the illuminated semicircles of intense bridge lighting. Billy knew that the season's swan song had begun and that it would be ended all too soon, all too abruptly. Still, several very large bass, non-resident, enormous fish had paused in their journey from the north, drawn to this final opportunity to fortify themselves for the energy-sapping journey that lay ahead. Instinct told them that when nature choreographed ideal conditions—as she surely would on this stark pre-winter night—they would be able to nourish themselves with virtually no expenditure of their own precious energy. Billy knew this as well.

Of the several huge stripers that positioned themselves strategically along the shadowline that very cold night, only one fish would be the object of Billy's focus. Using familiar reference points, he estimated her length at something over fifty-five inches; experience told him that he was dealing with a bass of equal, perhaps even greater actual weight. This fish could be a sixty.

A first cast.

The three-quarter ounce white bucktail plunked head-down into the blackness beyond the lighted perimeter of incandescence. Billy knew that these fish staged just below the surface, lying in wait for pods of fat-laden herring drawn to the surface glow of the bridge's lighting. He knew that these fish had no reason to stray from their adopted turf because they had no need to. They always waited for a meal to come to them. In the midst of nature's plenty, only a lure with very specific characteristics would have any chance of competing successfully for their attention. No "stock" product with a light enough head to flutter in the target zone just below the surface would carry a strong enough hook to hold one of these cows. Unadorned, moreover, it would never closely enough approximate resident baitfish to be taken seriously by any such late November bridgemonster. That is why, on chosen winter nights, Billy would spend much of his free time drilling out standard jig molds to accept far more substantial 8/0 hooks that the anemic 5/0's that were standard issue. Prior to presentation, a seven-inch strip of white porkrind completed the design. If all went as planned, the customized creation would present a silhouette that just might prove irresistible.

Immediately, Billy could see that the path of the cast lure actually might, just might, be perfect. He knew that the point of initial impact had little relation to the final position that it must attain if a strike were to be a possibility. His cast had to take into consideration every factor that could influence its trajectory and it had to do so at an absolutely precise point in time. He knew that with fish such as these, there might not be a second chance.

Prior to the critical moment, breathing stops. Then, in less than the space between heartbeats—the bucktail is gone.

Time becomes suspended. The entire outcome of this long and freezing night will now be defined by an ability to defy the compulsion of natural instinct. In the agonizing course of the longest split second that any fisherman will ever experience Billy must wait for the giant fish to close her mouth. Strike at this mistaken moment, with the intensity of force that must be employed to penetrate the jaw of such a monster and the lure will fly out, unobstructed, on the same rush of seawater upon which it entered microseconds earlier, snagging itself in a tangle somewhere on the iron railing of the bridge. But Billy has practiced this drill many times before. It takes everything in his being, but he waits.

"Like I said, if you're really a bridge fishermen—and there aren't many—everything will be visual. If you can't see what's happening every second you'll never be any good at this game. The fact that you're fishing at night is really what makes the whole thing possible. It's the intensity of the bright lights on the black water that sets up the scene. If you're fishing a white bucktail, it's gonna look like it's glowing in the dark. When it disappears in front of a 'log' you either have to sit on your own adrenaline rush until the fish closes her mouth or hope that the rocket that is launched back at you when you miss the fish won't end up stuck in your ear. If you're any good, in a split second you'll feel the fish move off with the tide—that's when you hit it with everything you've got. On this night in '78 that's precisely the way it happened. These are incredibly powerful fish that always run downtide when they're first hooked. That puts them **under** the bridge and a lot closer to freedom. They must be turned at this point or else you'll end up with just another bullshit story to tell your friends. The intense pressure will absolutely make you think that either the rod will break or the line will snap—which is always possible—but at a critical moment the fish will turn to ease the pressure and at that point, you've got a chance.

I always fish fifty pound line with a locked drag under these conditions because I know that there are no options. Turn the fish or lose the fish. Period. And if you think that all of this muscle tackle is giving the big, bad fisherman an unfair advantage against the poor, helpless fish—try it first and then let me know how you feel. Believe me, if you have the knowledge and the skill to be in the right place at the right time to hook one of these monsters you'll find out real fast that you're on **their** turf, not the other way around. I truly believe that very few guys could hang on to one of these cows long enough to ever see it up close.

But on this particular night, after an initial instinctive blast **under** the bridge this particular fish turned and headed into the ripping tide, hell bent on the inlet. I already knew this was a monster—the incredibly strong surges she made only convinced me that my eyes had not been wrong, up top. I worked the fish south, weaving my rod past the light poles and struggling more than I could remember in similar circumstances. On a high bridge as you move toward either shore the distance to the water diminishes—and that's when you pump in line. Getting a bridge fish to a bank and actually landing it is another story, but this fish eventually got there. I've slid a ton of fish up the rocks near bridges and every one gets my adrenaline going as I reach down to grab it. I never use a gaff, and I never miss a fish, but with this fish I wished I had one. In one quick motion my right thumb clamped into her mouth and I locked my fingers below in a vise grip.

I will not let go of a fish this way, not ever. I knew I had a high fifty and it seemed that I was now running on pure adrenaline. I dragged the fish high up into the safety of the reeds and raced back up top to see if a bigger member of this clan might be waiting. This had been my third fish that night. As the sky began to lighten, the bite ended and, as I suspected then, so did the season.

I don't keep many fish, but the one still in the reeds was heading for a certified scale. Actually, it ended up on two. Both readings were identical: sixty-four pounds, eleven ounces."

Although this photo doesn't do it justice, this **64** pound **11** ounce monster repesents Billy's best fish to date. Caught on a **New Moon** in November of 1978, it measured **54 1/2** inches in length and **32** inches in girth.

Few fishermen get the chance of ever seeing a fish like this in a lifetime.

Twenty-three years later, this fish remains Billy's personal best. In later years, three other fish were to come close, each between sixty and sixty-two pounds—but **I** knew that *The Greek* would not rest until the world's record had his name on it.

"The Beach Is Really
A Labor of Love"

The purity of the surf is undeniable and it is timeless.

THE OCEAN BEACHES OF LONG ISLAND are amazing in their ability to displace passing fashion, fad and circumstance with a stunning display of uncorrupted beauty. Drive south across the scattered islands of marsh into a rising sun, or into a setting sun—and the vinyl assault upon nature that is the mainland gradually leeches out of ones consciousness. Soon, we stand at the margins of time, held rapt by an unchanging sea, awed by her savage tenacity to endure.

Billy never calls me when the surf fishing is hot because he claims he's too focused on the fishing. Knowing what a psycho Billy is this may be true, but I tend to think he just can't overcome his compelling instinct to guard any mother lode that his fanaticism uncovers. Perhaps I am too harsh, though, because *The Greek* did call me the other night to invite me to the latest scene of the action.

It is mid June and the fish are on the beach.

Billy assures me that he will be in a certain spot at a certain time and that I will be able to locate him with relative ease (kind of like what they say about striped bass). He'll be fishing with one of his blood-oath buddies—one of those guys like the high priests guarding Akhenaton's tomb, who had their tongues cut out just in case they might talk in their sleep.

At the appointed hour I arrive and spot the van, just where it's supposed to be. A half-mile east on a deserted stretch of sand *Billy the Greek* and John (no moniker) are poised in anticipation of a strike. One-piece surf rods, eleven and ten feet long, respectively, are held almost vertically by each fisherman. The equipment is unusual, at least to me. The blanks are *Lamiglas Model 136 1MH's,* one of the heaviest sticks currently available on the market. There is nothing subtle about this tackle, not because *The Greek* likes to beat up the fish, but really for just the opposite reason.

"The beach is mainly a labor of love because you'll never have a lot of consistency catching fish in the suds. Sure, there will be blitzes every now and then, but relative to the number of hours invested, the surf's got to be the least productive method of taking fish. Still, I don't know a bass fisherman who doesn't get his biggest thrill out of hooking big stripers from the beach, and that's why none of us can really ever give it up. But remember, when it comes to selecting tackle, first and foremost you're at the beach to have the best possible chance of hooking the fish that may be there. If you're not going to use what it takes to get to the fish, then why bother? And getting to the fish usually means hefty rods capable of casting heavy baits with heavy sinkers out to and sometimes beyond an offshore bar. When the tide really runs and the wind really howls if you're not using eight to ten ounce *Hatteras* sinkers to anchor your chunks, you're at the beach for the scenery—because you're sure as hell not there to hook bass. Even if you're fishing artificials, whimpy rods and ultra-sophisticated light reels damn your chances before you even begin. And I'm sick of hearing about how using this tackle is unsportsmanlike. Plain and simple, I use the tackle that the circumstances call for—and that gives me the best chance of getting a good fish in while she still has the best chance of surviving. Playing out a bass for twenty minutes—no matter what method is used to catch it may be a lot of fun to some folks, but I guarantee you the fish will soon be dead if you release it. I release over ninety per-cent of my fish and they are almost always in good shape when they swim off. That's because I land fish quickly, usually with the intention of letting them go as soon as I realize that they're not going to better my season's best fish."

"No sand spikes?"

"Never, you'd never hook most of the fish that hit, and most of the time on the beach, they just don't hit that often. Would you believe that once during a really good bite not far from where we're standing, I watched a guy's rod nearly bend over double in a spike. By the time he got to it, guess what? So this same guy rebaits and spikes his rod again. Same thing. Talk about a slow learner—he misses a third hit! Meanwhile, me and John are slaughtering some really good size fish. *Mr. Meatball*, however, never did get the point. I mean I could understand not knowing all the details, but you gotta be brain dead not to get that message."

THE BREEZE IS southwest and the tide has just started to move in. Tufted clouds gather to the west behind a setting sun.

"The Beach is a labor of love."
Photo: courtesy Dick Mermon

They form a low scalene triangle of darkening cotton puffs, melded together. In the east the bright spark of a distant-flashing Fire Island Light is clearly visible—although a haze has camouflaged the needle tower itself and the other major structures that memory tells me are nearby.

The sky above the ocean in front of us is the deep blue of day's end.

Parallel to the beach just offshore at distances varying between fifty and seventy-five yards, tubular curls of white foam break on otherwise gentle seas. They mark the bars. Moving closer to the shore, larger waves build to surprising three-foot heights but do not break until they articulate their presence with a slapping textured thump that recedes in diminuendo, summoned by a mother ocean who pulls them back to her and never rests.

Billy sees the same majesty, but in a different way. He tells me how to read the beach, converting beauty into pragmatic detail. He freezes the scene into a transparent cross-section—like blocks of acrylic with suspended coins and golf balls in them that people use for paperweights —only here, the ocean and its life are suspended. Others do not see these particular revelations—they do not care to. It is enough for them to see the surf and clouds and feel the wind.

"A southwest breeze like this is good to learn almost any section of beach down here—it sets up breaking waves on the bars and leaves the deeper water flat so you can pretty much map out the travel and feeding lanes of the fish. The bars run parallel to the beach and the waves break over them because the water is more shallow above them. Baitfish move in through the deeper water breaks between the bars and the fish follow them through. When bait gets trapped between the bar and the shore, there's not much they can do to escape a feeding predator. Obviously, you always want to fish the bars or some other distinctive type of structure that holds or traps bait. Believe me, if there's no easy meal near by, no self-respecting striper has any reason to be there.

It really cracks me up to see how many guys come down to a beach and just set up anywhere as if the fish were put in the ocean just to come to them. They don't care about tides, wind direction, bait that's in the water or any of the other critical variables—they just figure they're entitled to catch fish. Anything is possible. If you keep coming down to the beach, sooner or later you will stumble into a feeding frenzy just like the ones they talk about in the magazine articles— complete with diving birds and frantic bait jumping out of the water with big bass on their tails. It happens, but don't hold your breath waiting. The surf is always tough and if you expect to be consistent you have to learn the details. The best guys in the world strike out in the suds more often than they score. And these are the guys who leave as little as possible to chance. They know that most of the time there will be no obvious indication of the presence of fish at all. They come down to the beach at every stage of the tide, even if they don't intend to fish. They memorize and map out all the features of the surf line that contribute to fishy conditions. And they know that these conditions are constantly changing. Sometimes bars disappear overnight, with or without any apparent reason. Just one major storm can change the potential of an entire beach. That's why it's crazy to think that any single guy can be a hotshot in every location. To me the biggest mistake made in fishing is to think you can possibly become an expert everywhere. Let's be serious. With the amount of specific knowledge that is essential to consistently catch big striped bass, one of the most selective fish in the ocean, you'd better learn how to specialize. Locate a few good spots. Learn them cold. Fish them hard. Or pick up a six-pack and grab the remote."

"Billy," I ask, "how well do you know **this** stretch of beach?"

"Like the back of my hand, Mike."

"And those bunker you've been surgically dissecting—they're so fresh that you could resuscitate them with a little CPR, right?"

"They're fresher than I was in Miss Giardi's history class in junior high."

"So, *El Greco*, oh legend in your own mind—everything tonight seems to be perfectly aligned with the gospel according to Legakis. Perhaps, then, you could share with me what has happened to the fish on this most wondrous evening."

"Yes, my old buddy, you're right—I could—but then I'd have to kill you."

AS WELL AS I thought I knew Billy, I had to accept a possibility that I never really considered before: Billy is sometimes left with no choice but to put fish before friends. This is not to say that *The Greek* was ever incapable of being a true-blue, to-the-death comrade—but that he is fully capable of drawing a line with friendship when it comes to very big fish with stripes.

I have always appreciated Billy's poetic license in recounting the specifics of impressive catches (or purported strikeouts) concerning his own efforts. After all, it is not an easy thing to subjugate ego to secrecy. We all want our moment in the sun. But I have come to understand that Billy is perfectly willing to live in the shade, even to subsist in total darkness the rest of his days, if it means increasing his odds with a world's record-class bass. The math is simple. There just aren't very many of these fish—but there are huge numbers of fisherman who would do almost anything to get a shot at one. You can't blame a guy, especially an obsessive nut-job like Billy, for wanting to keep the odds in his favor. All's fair they say…

At this point in my life, I write for a living. I like to catch fish for fun. But I don't have to catch fish to live (and I mean **live**, not "earn a living"). Billy knows this, so I guess I shouldn't be insulted if what he really does on the occasions when he allows me to accompany him is to humor me. Billy on the other hand lives to catch big striped bass—and I truly believe he must continue do so in order to live. Anyone who knows Billy well knows that this is true and should never be offended by things that might get lost in the translation whenever he chooses to "share" his knowledge with you. If you are anything less than a fanatic-in-arms, or even if you are touched in the same portion of the brain as *The Greek*, there will always be a very good chance that "incoming" might really mean "outgoing," that "southwest" might really mean "northeast," and that "it sucks" might really mean that huge fish have never been so hungry in their lives.

You Don't Get More Than One Chance

CTUALLY, THE LINE WAS ONLY A FEW DAYS OLD, but it had already done its part in helping to land over a dozen good-sized fish. Billy positioned the spool of fifty-pound test within the frame of the *Squidder* and locked down the thick red side plate of the reel. Now the line was brand new. One small step perhaps, but a step that could prove critical, later.

Most fish had long departed the rapidly chilling waters of *Jones Inlet,* following the unmarked passageway of bait and water temperature to their winter grounds. Only very large blue-back herring still found conditions to their liking—only very large blue-back herring and exceedingly large striped bass and Billy.

The challenge was formidable: match the forage with something artificial, something made of lead and hair and paint; caress it past the nose of one of nature's marvels of pure instinct and proven survivability—and overcome the startling power of such a fish in its own natural environment. Most importantly, don't allow adrenaline to fuck up everything the years have taught you. Definitely, that was the most important.

Billy knew the drill. He had practiced it many times before—the sixty-four, eleven, the sixty-two, the two sixties. But this fish was different. **This fish was longer than the width of the shadow line that extended below him, a shadow line whose dimensions were etched in his brain.** This fish had to go seventy, or even eighty plus. It wasn't the cold, it wasn't fatigue, and although he might have been more excited than he had been over any other fish in his lifetime, it wasn't the excitement. It was objective fact. This fish was longer than the width of the shadow line. It wasn't an apparition. It was marine biology. This fish had to go well over seventy pounds.

At that point in time such a monster could suck down as many fat, fragrant, energy-packed herring as she wanted to. Without effort, without fanfare. There was little likelihood that she would actually elect to eat the proffered artificial offering. Billy knew that his only hope was to somehow intimidate this incredibly wise hunter, to suddenly introduce a presence that might, by its very intrusion, provoke a synapse of response.

"Fish like this have a unique casualness about them. They're not afraid of a lure. They will merely turn their head aside, completely unaffected by what they recognize as something unworthy of their attention. They have an arrogance that I believe demonstrates a real intelligence. People always ask me if I think striped bass actually think, or if their behavior is just purely instinctive. I know what fish do. It's some of the people I've met that I'd ask that particular question about."

The lure was a white, two-ounce arrowhead bucktail with a hefty seven-inch strip of white porkrind attached. The hair had been substantially lengthened in order to make the package come closer to replicating the large herring that drew these huge *late cruisers* to the bridge that night.

The incoming tide was now rushing in with an intensity that carved distinct eddies behind the bridge supports where they penetrated the water. The breeze was northwest at about fifteen. The monster had not moved.

"I took my first cast about twenty feet in front of this fish, at a point where I knew that my lure would be swept directly into her feeding zone. But I never tried to fool myself. With a fish that had survived to that size I knew it would take more than the perfect cast with the perfect lure to get her to show interest. I knew that she would know my lure wasn't real. I had to get her to abandon a lifetime of cautiousness to hit a target that all her instincts told her to ignore."

The bucktail was positioned perfectly. Billy lifted his rod tip high to keep the lure from sinking below the strike zone. All big fish at the bridge suspended themselves just below the surface as they waited for their victims. Just as the artificial offering drifted into the crosshairs, the cow calmly turned her massive head slightly to the right. Yes! Yes!—No, damn it, no! No reaction other than the slight, bored body motion that Billy had come to recognize as a sure sign of total disinterest in such a fish. The bucktail swept impotently away on the tide, disappearing quickly beneath the bridge.

"True, I was excited when I saw this fish—but that didn't stop me from doing everything right. I was deadly meticulous. I took my time, because I knew I had time. You always have a choice. You can get your bait to the fish as quick as possible without checking every detail first (but chances are you'll either never get a hit because the lure will be wrong, or the presentation will be wrong or something will be wrong that will spook the fish—or if by some miracle you hook the fish, you'll drop it because of bad line, or a bad knot or bad something) or you can do everything to put the odds in your favor and hope the fish will wait. Experience has told me that ninety-nine times out of a hundred, the fish will be there when you're ready, unless you went out for breakfast first or something.

The way this fish was aligned in the current, I thought that I was going to hook the world's record striped bass that night. The way a fish is set up in the shadow line of a bridge tells me a lot. This fish really looked like it might go for my lure if I did absolutely everything right. O K, so I was wrong. She wasn't interested in my first cast, a cast I executed to imitate the herring she was stuffing herself with throughout the first part of the tide. I should have known better. This was no desperate fish. This fish was uncanny—smart, mature, well-fed and, most of all, experienced. If I was to have any chance with this monster, I would have to appeal to a stronger instinct than hunger—I would have to get her to strike out at the audacious infringement of my lure upon her exclusive domain. She would have to strike out of arrogance, she would have to strike out of pride."

BILLY RE-EVALUATED the situation. The fish had not changed position at all. He knew that repeated casts to the same spot would serve no practical purpose—they would, in fact, diminish his chances of success with each subsequent attempt. At this point, practice was definitely not going to make perfect. He saw himself as a big-league pitcher going head to head with a big-league batter. The more "pitches" the fish got to "see," the less likelihood there was that the "batter" would be fooled. He had to intimidate this fish.

The second cast was positioned with a very slight adjustment that would carry the lure a few degrees off to the right-side of the bass. Given her dominion over that precise piece of watery turf, given the speed of the current, given the perceived intrusion of this foreign object into her private realm—she might respond on instinct, and nothing but instinct, alone. It was Billy's only hope.

The lure had been changed to a dark color old-style Alou *Cow-Killer* that sometimes worked when nothing else would. The technique was more aggressive—the bait-tail darting higher and faster, barely encroaching into the peripheral vision of the monster. Then, in the smallest possible fragment of time, the first flash of hope—a heart-stopping vibration of pectoral fins, the inevitable and fatal precursor to a strike—followed by, followed by—nothing, by nothing at all. In his heart at that point in time Billy knew that this fish was not to be taken on this November night, under this new November moon.

"The fish remained in the same position, unchanged, after my third and final cast. At that point I knew that any additional cast would be useless. I watched her for another twenty minutes. It was really a sight to behold. A black velvet study in motionless independence. Twenty minutes without so much as moving more than an inch or two in either direction. Calm and relaxed is how I would describe her. It was really something to see.

As the tide began to slow, she just sank down into the darkness and I could see her, as she emerged from the shadow line into the band of bridge light. She just swam off. She just swam off."

Just Put An "X" On
The Side of Your Boat

W E HUMANS ARE INDEED A MODEST LOT, remark-
ably confident and comfortable with our superiority to every other life form attempting to
scratch out an existence on our shared patch of real estate.
Obviously it wasn't always that way. We arrived at this state
of audacious self-delusion only after concluding that we
were generally better—even more powerful, in many
instances—than nature.

While outer space may have been the "final frontier" of
the late twentieth century, the oceans' inner space was never
far behind. All the *GPS* numbers in the book, all the inte-
grated circuits in Silicon Valley, can't really change that. It is
this abiding mystery of the sea that withholds knowledge
from most of us—and it is this very knowledge that will
always separate the men from the boys on the water.

For Billy and the endangered handful of remaining
practitioners of his type of fanaticism, it is fortunate that so
many "fisherman" now entrust their success to the dictates
of marine electronics. They flip switches and study liquid
crystal displays. They wait. And as these marvels of fishing

technology specify the parameters of success, guys like Billy look to the tides and the wind and the bait, look to the surface movement of the waters in the bays, look to the angle of the drift—look to the life cycle of the seas—to locate and catch big striped bass, and catch them with amazing consistency, and catch them where all the electronics in the shop say no such fish exist.

One morning about five years ago Billy called asking me to go out with him on a brand new boat he had just taken delivery on. The twenty-one footer was beautiful—powerful, fast and sea-worthy. *The Greek* showed up with several CIA-looking aluminum attaché cases which contained the latest in marine electronics, each cradled in the bosom of expensive-looking, custom-molded protective foam. He showed me how each device fit like a glove into the various niches that had been customized in the instrument console to accommodate them. I was treated to a digitized display of streaming *GPS* numbers, continuously changing bottom contours and assorted electronic pings.

We took the boat out and flew through the open bay at skin-stinging speeds. Billy maneuvered the vessel with accustomed skill as the electronic read-outs flickered in shades of orange, red and amber. It was obvious that this was not to be a fishing trip, but a combination shake-down and "impress Mike" cruise. Mission accomplished. I was impressed. This was not what I had been accustomed to with Billy, but I was definitely impressed.

It was several months before I heard from Billy again. Did I want to go bass fishing? The plan, a spontaneously-generated one it seemed, was to fish locally in mid-morning at a spot that was atypically, for *The Greek,* located in one of the busiest areas of the bay. Billy must be real bored. But, why not? Billy had shut me up more times than I would like to admit.

We met at the boat at ten. I was surprised by the conspicuous absence of the "CIA" briefcases. Had Billy been foolish enough to permanently install his expensive electronic equipment on the boat where it would surely prove irresistible to thieves in the night. His boat slip, after all, was totally unprotected.

"No, I leave all that shit home now. A waste of time and effort, even though I have to admit it looks real pretty."

Other than engine gauges, the only high tech device now in evidence was a small, round digital depth meter with nothing more dramatic than a numerical read-out. The customized instrument brackets and cut-outs stood barren, devoid of their technological accoutrements.

"When I got the new boat I wanted it outfitted from the ground up to meet my specific needs. Once they were taken care of, the complete electronics package kind of went along for the ride. I don't want you to get me wrong on this. High-tech has its place, especially way offshore, but the more you get into the habit of staring at digital readouts, the more you start to believe that your own instincts can't be trusted. Once that happens, it's time to hang it up and hit the rocking chair. I don't know a single fisherman who produces results that is anything but an instinctive animal. Every great fisherman— every great pin-hooker, haul-seiner, party boat or charter captain, surfcaster, or offshore specialist—I don't give a damn who—cannot be great without first having superior natural instincts to begin with, trusting them, and then following them. If I had twenty bucks for every guy that has run over schools of big fish while his eyes were glued to an assortment of digital read-outs, I'd be a rich man today. I mean, tell me, who do you think would catch more—let's say, codfish and bigger ones—the guy in the million dollar sportsfisherman with every piece of electronics on the market, or *Captain Al* running with nothing in the wheel house but a compass and a clock? Do you want me to tell you about sharpshooters in fourteen-foot tin boats who came back to the docks with bass that would bring tears to your eyes? Do you ever wonder why the *Posey* haul-seining crews out east remain legends to this day, when all they relied on for their consistent production from one generation to the next was a manifestation of nothing more than something found in their own DNA? If you want to be a fisherman—a real fisherman—you have to understand the life cycle of the ocean. You have to comprehend that you live on the land, you don't live in the sea—you just visit it for a while. You have to understand that the conditions that hold fish are never forever, they are constantly changing. Great fisherman all possess the ability to comprehend this and to constantly adjust their methods and techniques accordingly. If you're not born with this sixth sense, you have to learn to develop it or you'll never be great. And you have to work at it every day in some way, whether you're on the water or not."

Billy eased the boat into position no more than two hundred feet from the shore, aligning ranges and admonishing me to be ready with the "first anchor."

"First anchor—does that imply that there's a second anchor—because I don't see one."

"In the locker with the first one! Have the second hook ready to go when I give you the word!"

"I hate to ruin your day, old man, but there's only one anchor in here."

"*Meatballs*—my life is filled with *meatballs*—take the wheel a minute and just hold her where she is."

"Son of a bitch—Jeff must have lost the second fucking anchor on his last trip and never replaced it. I swear I'll cut off his balls the next time I see the bastard!"

"So what's the big deal, you still have an anchor to use."

"If we single-anchor in this tide with this breeze we will swing like a gate. The only time we even might get fish is when we swing over the piece I wanted to sit on top of.

Son of a bitch!"

The whole scenario seemed wrong to me. Ten-thirty in the morning. Bright sun. Setting up just to the south of what looked like a major traffic lane for pleasure boats on Great South Bay. I waited for the next move.

The Greek watched the digital depth indicator. As barren as this stretch of outboard-churned water looked to me, it must have looked or smelled or just plain felt like the real thing to Billy. My senses cried *skunk*—his instincts spelled *bass*.

Scores of very serious looking fishing craft, their antennae swaying, their radar rotating, sped off east, then south, in their quest for trophies. I watched as magnificent vessels disappeared into the persistent haze of late morning.

When the depth gauge read *22,* I lowered the anchor, as instructed. We dropped back until the orange numerals indicated what Billy obviously considered the magic readout of *26.* I snubbed the line off on the bow cleat.

"It's the only modern miracle I always leave running because it makes things a little easier, especially when I can't pick up good ranges. But the truth is I can set up directly over any piece in the bay without any electronic wizards on board at all. If fact, I know I do better without them because I don't get distracted when it's just me concentrating on what I know.

And no one had a clue!
The swirl from a monster striper went totally unnoticed by other speeding boats as ***BTG*** let the fish just sit.
This was bright sun at mid-morning!

I love to watch guys come up on coordinates they more than likely bought from someone—a piece loaded with fish—and not be able to anchor the boat so it will sit over the hot spot. They'll be dropping prime baits down to fish that may be only a few feet away but never move off the place they call home. These guys have the equipment, they have the locations—but they never have the fish because they lack the most fundamental understanding of the relationship between their boat and the sea. They lack the required instincts and refuse to invest the time and effort it takes to develop them. Which means that they will accidentally catch fish once in a while, but they'll never be any good. This type of comedy always reaches the max when these guys find themselves in the miserable situation of having to watch real fisherman bail the shit out of fish at a real tight location while they watch in total frustration. I half expect them to throw their rods overboard like in the scene from the TV commercial when the golfer throws his expensive clubs into the lake. Yeah, it can be an actual joy to behold.

And the lesson, my son? Yes—if you want to be good, pay your own dues, develop your own instincts, catch your own fish."

I was thinking that I could actually swim to shore, and I wasn't a good swimmer. Why were we here? The boat with no name swung gently in the current. Billy rigged two conventional outfits with fish finders and hung nice cross-sections of fresh bunker on each.

"Pretty big baits for porgies, aren't they Billy—or are we fishing for sea bass?"

"Everyone's a comedian! Just let your rig walk back from the boat about fifty feet, put it in free spool with the clicker on and put it in the rod holder. I know you don't like to exert yourself holding a big, heavy rod for a long time and it may actually be a few minutes before we get a bite. Besides, the rod holder probably has a better chance of actually hooking a fish than you do."

"Should be seeing something soon—as soon as we swing over…"

"Click…click, click, click." I swear, just like the scene from *Jaws*. "Click…click…ka—lklklklklk" with no spaces in between clicks now, instantly accelerating into the loud metallic buzz that is unmistakable whenever you hear it.

"Grab the rod and hook the frigging fish."

It was apparently hooked already and took off for points east with conviction.

"Don't make such a fucking show of it or the guy's seeing eye dog in the boat going by will bark loud enough for him to stop by and pay us a visit. Just bring the fish to the stern and I'll grab him. You're acting like you've got a monster on. These are not giant fish—just reel him in."

Damn, this was a good fish. I couldn't estimate how good because the biggest bass I had ever caught up to that point was hooked in the middle of a freezing night on a party boat not far from where we were at that very moment—and I was so numb at three in the morning that I couldn't tell much about anything. That fish turned out to be a twenty-eight pounder. This fish sure as hell had to be bigger—much bigger, it seemed to me—a "forty-five" or even the elusive "fifty." A few minutes later, *El Greco* unceremoniously hoisted a beautiful, shining striper into the boat. "Thirty-five, thirty-six" was his assessment.

That remained to be proven later, for the trip was not yet over. I'll eliminate the drama and symphony of clicks,

BTG and Mike with local fish taken right near home.
Some beautiful fish among the dozens that were caught.

though, and get to the bottom line. I quickly hooked another fish, got even more excited, suffered even more of Billy's verbal abuse—and dropped the obvious monster for "playing with him too much." While admiring the first beauty, still quite alive but lying with characteristic stillness on the deck, would you believe that the clicker goes off again? Same drill. The fish pretty much hooks herself, rips off a short burst of line and proceeds to fight with heavy, pronounced thumps that bend the rod tip into the water with her first few surges of unmistakable power.

But Billy doesn't like to make a show of things. I want recognition of my obvious superior fish-catching abilities. I want to bask in the glow of the full noonday sun illuminating not just a pair of turn-you-green-with-envy stripers (that I begged Billy to keep), but also the extraordinary angler who has accomplished what lesser men might consider impossible (or at least highly unlikely) under such conditions. But no, "if I wanted to continue this relationship" I had to be satisfied with a very private sense of accomplishment—made possible through the uncanny instincts and skill of this eccentric half-fish character who had once again made me eat my own admonitions of incredulity.

To this day, two things about that trip will never cease to amaze me: first, that no one else had a clue as to what was going on that crazy, late-summer morning—and, second, just as *The Greek* had predicted, each of the three fish hooked in that span of no more than forty-five minutes hit at almost the exact moment that Billy said they would. Now that's the kind of sixth sense you'll never be able to buy at any specialty store.

And lest I forget to mention it, the two boated fish weighed in at thirty-six and thirty-seven pounds—just like my humble comrade had said they would.

I Really Don't Ask Much

THE NEXT TIME YOU COME DOWN HERE, it wouldn't kill you to bring along a couple of fucking containers of coffee, would it?"

It was clearly a statement, phrased as a question in an extraordinarily rare concession to something resembling civility. I hadn't been out on the beach with *The Greek* in many years but that was no excuse for forgetting the October night chill, the magic of coffee and the *Gospel According to Billy*.

THE SURF AT night. When the sky is clear the cold air turns the heavens into crystal hardness. There are stars that don't exist just three miles to the north and sounds too delicate to survive the short journey home. If there were never any fish, for most of us the scene itself would be much more than enough. In a fleeting moment of barely emergent sensitivity *The Greek* begins to articulate agreement—before a distinct bump in the night shocks him back to a less sentimental reality.

For some time I realized that if I were to continue my attempts to chronicle the exploits of my erratic fishing mentor, I would have to supplement my past observations with

108 • Michael G. Cinquemani

significant new first-hand accounts. How else could I authenticate what would otherwise be dismissed as pure bullshit. But I knew that pinning Billy down would not be easy. By definition, secrecy was part of the game, as was the ability to relocate to where the fish were at any given moment in time. To that end we had devised a loosely-structured system to help me track down Billy on the beach that fall. It's success hinged on the fact that *The Greek* has always been a strong believer in specialization—learning a limited number of highly fishable areas cold rather than blindly chasing around unfamiliar waters in hope of hitting a bonanza. For this season that meant that Billy would repeatedly fish only three or four possible locations running along the southern beaches of the Island from *West End Two* to *Gilgo*. The plan was for Billy to phone me ahead of time with the *most probable* starting point of a trip. At six-thirty, say, he would *probably* be at *Field Six*. If not *Six*, then *probably Gilgo*. If not *Gilgo* … You get the idea. *Probably*. Find the truck in a specific parking lot, near a particular beach entrance, and I would *probably* find *The Greek*. Mind you, for Billy this was close to giving up the location of the *Lost Ark of the Covenant*. For me, it meant a lot of hunting and pecking in the dark—but it actually worked more often than it didn't.

On moonless nights the visibility along the beach isn't very good and just spotting Billy is a challenge in itself. But the secret "truck orientation code" has tipped me off as to the direction in which to walk. To avoid the extra effort of trudging through soft, deep sand I move along the water's edge, gladly trading dampened feet for the more resilient pathway of sand compacted by receding waves. Battery-powered lights glow at intervals, illuminating baits, or knots, or friends. But none of the figures is Billy. I think I'm walking in the right direction but the process is hit or miss, at best. I don't want to shine my *MagLite* in less-than-appreciative faces, but neither do I want to shout out, "Billy is that you?" These guys all look the same. The question is, "Where's the phantom leader?"

Then I remember. Find the guy who's not wearing the waders. And, sure enough, there's Billy, a half mile west of the middle tunnel. Tonight he's fishing with his latest, protegee, Jamie. Others have been cloned from *The Greek,* and in daylight the similarity of their equipment to his would lead one to reasonably conclude that a high-end tackle manufacturer had run a fire sale on identical surf rigs. Imitation is what, they say?

Billy is bemoaning the fact that he has missed "the bite." While several decent fish had been caught along the beach prior to his arrival at sunset this night, *The Greek* has left work a little later than instinct told him he should and things have now gone completely dead. Billy had given Jamie the coordinates of where to fish and just before *The Greek's* arrival he has landed a real nice fish which was secreted away to avoid an instantaneous rise in popularity.

Now, suddenly, out of nowhere—a "bump."

Billy whipped the eleven and a half foot surf stick back hard and then insisted on handing me the rod once its arch made it clear that a respectable fish had inhaled the fresh bunker chunk. I really didn't want someone else hooking a fish for me but the excitement of the moment got to me. I grabbed the rod. The fish was taking line and I was soon taking abuse. I don't think I had half a dozen small surf-caught bass to my credit up to that point in my life and here was this fish buzzing fifty-pound test *Ande* off a heavy set drag on a *Squidder* in startling spurts of surprising power. I was excited. I was impressed. So what if I wasn't actually poetry in motion?

"You're not going to break the rod. You're not going to

break the line. It's just a fish and not a very big one—just crank him in, Mike!"

"Billy, you're wrong this time. This is a good fish. He keeps taking line. How can I crank in the fish if he's running?"

"Gee, I don't know. Maybe the same way I crank in *forties* and *fifties* with the same outfit in less time than you've had that baby on and without the *Academy Award* winning performance. OK, OK—I forgot that I'm dealing with a full-blown *museum piece*. OK, then go for the 'lights, camera, action' approach—but try to get him in before our brethren down the beach cast their spotlights on us and conclude that there may still be some hope of catching a decent fish tonight."

"Right! He's seems to be coming in now, but I have no idea where he is. Can you see him?"

"See him? I've been watching that fish for the past five minutes. He's almost in the wash right now. Just crank the line tight and walk straight backwards. I'll do the rest."

And Billy did the rest, as usual. No boots, no waders. No light. No gaff, no net, no nothing. He just calmly hopped down, sneaker-clad, to the water's edge and came walking back with his hand under what seemed to me to be a very large gill cover. That's how Billy lands all his fish, no matter what the size. That's why, at the end of a season, Billy's hands look like he's been doing personal battle with a *John Deere* harvester.

The fish was long and lean, motionless, beautiful. It smelled fresh, almost like a summer melon. And it looked pretty damn big to me. I've always had a problem with keeping any fish, but especially big and impressive ones.

"Not bad, Mike. And you didn't do such a pathetic job after all, either. Congratulations. Nice fish. Really. Skinny for this time of year, though. Twenty-four, twenty-five. You like fish, don't you? You want to keep him to eat?"

Emotions aside, I did. To eat, yes, but also to flaunt. I doubted that I would ever develop Billy's extraordinary ability to satisfy himself with the gratification of the catch, alone. I needed the glory, even if I'd done little, if anything, to deserve it. This would always remain a tough issue for me.

"The pattern may be changing. The last few nights they hit at the top of the incoming. We might have them on the outgoing now. I don't think that your fish was just a stray. With the wind southeast we're getting some pretty good wave action. We're fishing right at the opening of the inshore bar here. Bait's getting swept out pretty good now—and the fish will be cruising this location for an easy meal. I'd expect some kind of action for the next hour or so. Not a big school—but maybe some big fish."

"Here we go!" It was Jamie, just steps to my left.

Jamie was Billy's current brother-in-arms, a dyed-in-the-wood disciple of *The Greek* whose tenacity for striped bass fishing made him worthy of learning from the master, himself. Jamie utilized the same surf rig as Billy; he steaked chunks of bunker from the same cache of sushi-quality baitfish, and he fished the very same productive locations, more often than not, alongside the mentor who had taught him so much.

Jamie hit the fish hard. I gave him room, sensing immediately that this was a hot one. Even with my limited striped bass catching knowledge the first signs seemed unmistakable. The rod took on a beautiful, slowly throbbing arc; line spurted off the *Squidder* in substantial quantities that far exceeded the amounts taken by my fish, just minutes before. I've caught a few really big fish in my day—from large fluke to giant bluefin tuna—and the really big ones always seem to act the same way once they're hooked. You sense their power right away. Jamie's fish had that look— the look of unpanicked strength—but it didn't have it for long. No more than a minute into the fight, the fifty pound test mono simply snapped. Billy said it was at the knot. Makes sense, but who knows?

And Jamie?

He's in mourning. I mean, really upset. He'd done everything right, everything à la Billy; fresh line, perfect equipment, proper technique, *yadda, yadda*. But he's convinced he's lost his first *fifty* and it will take him even longer than I might have imagined to recover his composure.

"Jamie had a nice fish, but it wasn't any monster. Gotta add at least five or ten pounds to a fish you never see. Yeah, mighta had a forty. Popped off at the knot. Not to worry— he'll get over it. Some big fish here on the outgoing, though."

Jamie's back in the water, still upset. I don't know him well enough to really give him a hard time about his fish so I just agree that it looked real good to me. But he's really pissed, convinced that he screwed up somewhere. We leave him to talk things over with himself. You know, get right back up on the horse…

"There's a fish!"
Whack, whack…mega whack! I mean, there ain't going to be any doubt that this bass is hooked. Whatever I said

about Jamie's fish clearly applies to Billy's new adversary. There's the same sense of formidable mass and power, the same "I ain't going nowhere" show of resistance. Only this is *BTG* and this guy has some pretty inflexible ideas about who's got whom on the hook.

Within no more than three minutes *The Greek* is at the wash and the third striped bass of the night, our limit that I have convinced Billy to keep, is being dragged up high on the sand. Laid next to my earlier fish there seems to be no basis for comparison, other than the stripes and a general anatomical similarity. Billy's fish dwarfs "mine" not only in length, but most impressively, in girth. This fish's head is huge and the belly is enormous. Jamie goes to retrieve the bass that he had caught prior to our arrival and it, too, is an impressive fish. It is almost as long as Billy's, but lacks quite the same measurements around. These two fish, however, are very similar—very big. Billy estimates them at "forty, maybe forty-five." I am ecstatic and suggest that we take some pictures. The camera, not normally a part of the gear that is carried to the beach is in Jamie's truck. I get to fulfill my destiny on this trip by "volunteering" to make the hike back to the parking lot. There's no way either of these two guys is leaving his post. On my return, twenty minutes later, we record the fish for posterity. Although Billy gets another hit, the bite seems to be over on the dropping tide. Quite a night. But not quite over yet.

"OK, guys, how do we get these fish back to the vehicles?"

"I call my valet, Mike, and he runs down here with a wheelbarrow. Duh. How the fuck do you think we get them back?"

Tobay was "dead," but Billy got a **45** and your author landed a **26.** Jamie (not seen) had a **42.** Not bad for an area that was reported to be holding "no fish" at the time.

Tobay forty-five pounder with fresh bunker used for reference.
Fall, 2001.

Billy and Jamie get their gear together and then each flips his fish over his right shoulder. Clouds have started to move in from the south and flashes of lightening far, far in the distance backlight them at intervals in eerie puffy glows of incandescence.

"If you wedge the fish in near your neck and find the balance point, front, back just right, the fish weighs almost nothing."

"I'd rather wait for your valet, Billy. How the fuck can the fish weigh nothing, no matter where the hell you wedge it?"

"Try it. You'll see what I mean."

It didn't work out exactly the way these guys said it would, but eventually we made it back to the cars without my going into full cardiac arrest. It was only about eleven o'clock on this mild and still starry night, beautiful beyond description. Ours were the only three vehicles left in the parking lot.

Billy's fish measured forty-nine and a half inches long and weighed forty-five pounds on a *Chatillon* scale. Jamie's fish weighed forty-two pounds and "my" runt went twenty-six—my biggest surf-caught bass to date. And that was the end of the show—for no one else, by oath, was to see these fish in the flesh.

THE FOLLOWING WEEKEND I went down to a local, well-stocked bait and tackle shop to snoop around and listen to a little of the local scuttlebutt. Reports of terrific bass fishing had been circulating everywhere—so much so that obvious neophytes were out in force, shopping for fresh bunker and live eels to cash in on the easy pickings. It was one-thirty in the afternoon. A serious fisherman, an obvious "regular" came in, speaking the kind of fishing code recognized only by the limited confraternity of serious bass hounds.

"Did you hear about the fish John got on Thursday?"

"Yeah, he brought it in on Friday. It was a real nice fish—one of the better fish I've seen this season."

I ask, rather sheepishly, "How big was that fish—the one that that guy John caught, anyway?"

"It was a real nice fish. I weighed it in. Weighed just over thirty pounds. Thirty pounds, mind you, not thirty inches."

"Wow, that is a real nice fish! I'll bet you don't see them that big very often. Over thirty pounds. That is a real nice fish."

It was an interesting visit to the tackle shop that afternoon, and it taught me something very important about striped bass fishing. The next time that I'm scheduled to meet Billy on the beach—or on the boat or at the bridge for that matter—believe me, I won't make the mistake of forgetting the coffee again.

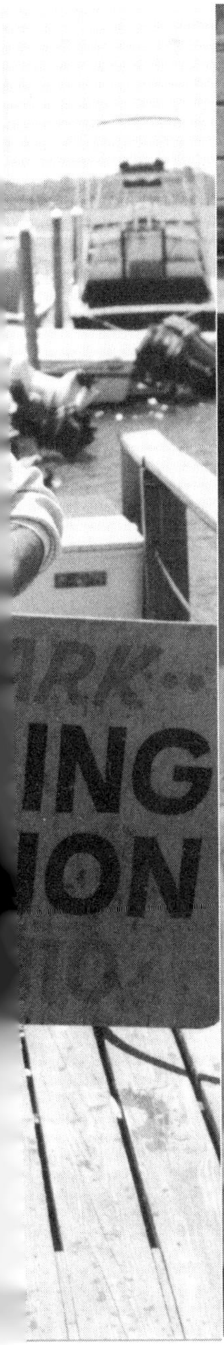

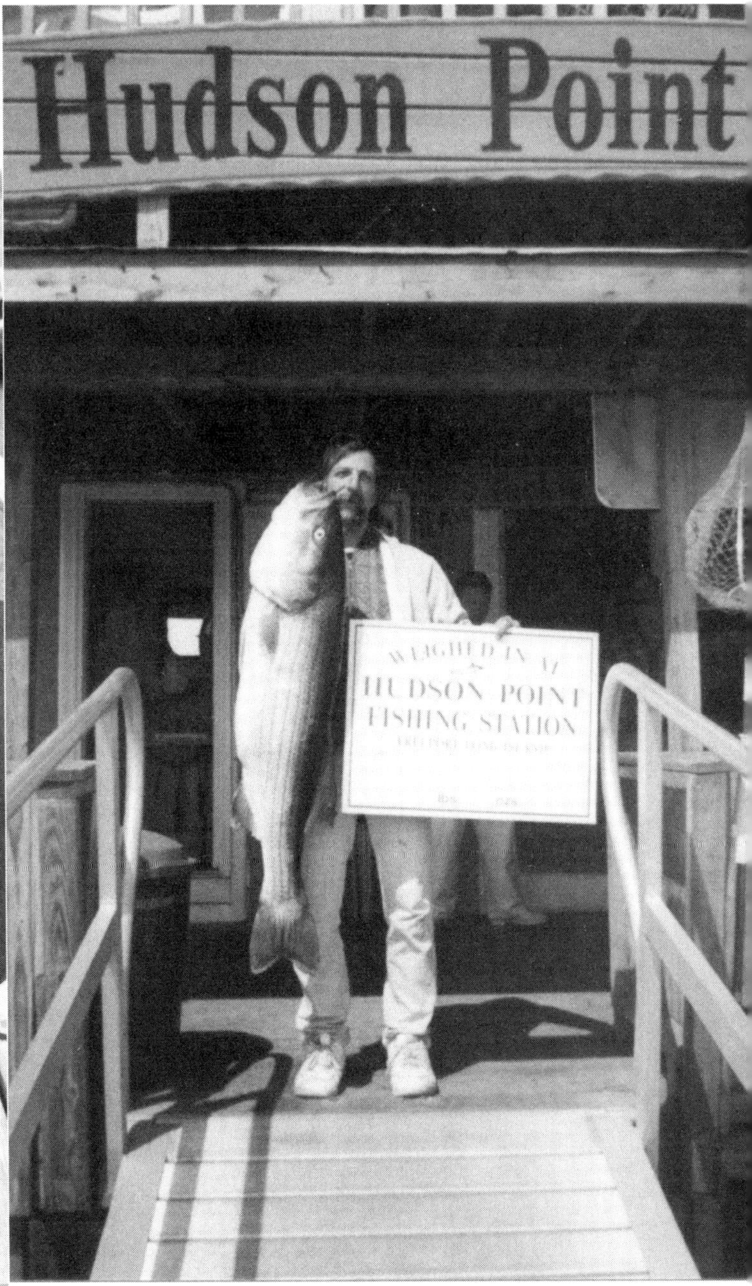
Hudson Point
WEIGHED IN AT
HUDSON POINT
FISHING STATION

BILLY TELLS ME that you can always tell the kind of season he's having by the condition of his hands. This fall his hands are in really bad shape. That's good.

We are anchored on one of Billy's hot spots not ten minutes from the biggest party boat fleet on the Island. We are not hidden by night nor shrouded by fog. Although we're well into the fall, private boats by the dozens fly by or prowl in the immediate vicinity. Given the distinct chill of the freshening breeze, we assume these are pretty much all fishermen targeting striped bass. Most boats whiz off to areas highlighted in the latest fishing reports. Many slow down to scope us out— only because we look like we're serious about something. Some just pull right up to us and drop their baits in the water. Few remain for long. I see no fish taken by any of them.

It's nine-thirty in the morning and in the last two hours we have released sixteen striped bass weighing between twenty and thirty-two pounds. A thirty-five pounder, promised to a non-fishing friend for the table, resides in the fishbox. This fish was deeply hooked and had little chance of survival. Billy has "landed" each of these bass in exactly the same way. Once the fish nears the boat he simply grabs it from the lower jaw. There is never a gaff, never a net—neither can even be found on board. He rarely brings a fish into the boat, but removes the hook, instead, with its body still in the water.

Virtually every fish Billy catches is hooked in the side of its jaw. Almost every fish I catch is hooked deeper into the fish's gullet. Both types of hookups are reversed with an equal degree of surgical dispatch and precision by *The Greek*. And this all takes a terrible toll on his hands.

Billy is a powerful guy. I've seen him crank in a dozen big bass in rapid succession without breathing hard. I've seen him walk a mile through soft sand with a fifty-pound striper over his shoulder. I've even seen him flip my fish over his other shoulder when he figured that I was about to drop dead and then trek the distance to his van under the combined weight of seventy pounds of striped bass.

But nowhere is Billy's strength more evident than in his hands.

Billy has often spoken of the infamous *Legakis* vise-grip. It has always reminded me of stories I had heard about big snapping turtles, whose heads would have to be severed before they would release the jaw-lock on their prey. Billy has told me that he never lets go of a fish—never. But hearing and seeing are two different things. I have witnessed the technique, believe me, more times that I have ever needed to in order to dispel any residual incredulity I might once have harbored. Some day I expect to hear about a startled fisherman catching a huge striper, not with a lure or a hook still attached, or an entire surf outfit in tow, but with *The Greek's* hand still clamped down on its lower jaw, tendons streaming enticingly behind in a display of ultimate irony.

Landing the fish is one thing, unhooking him, another.

Popping a hook from the bony vertex of a big striper's jaw —strictly without the use of tools—is clearly a talent, but not necessarily an act of advanced surgical acumen. Even though I have personally witnessed many experienced fishermen struggle against such a task, it's a skill that can be acquired. Not by me, mind you, but by many.

"… before the bass realizes what has happened,
she's swimming back from whence she came."
Photo courtesy: **The Long Island Fisherman**/Dick Mermon

But consider the opportunity for battle damage, even in this less demanding scenario. True, this is not a monster bluefish, with dental work poised to sever arteries. But one hand still gets raked by the abrasive rasp of the upper and lower jaws, while the other stands to get sliced by bone or gill plate. That's if all goes well and the fish cooperates. If not, there's always the chance of collateral damage from spines—or sometimes from the instrument of capture, itself. If the fish has been hooked deeply, there is absolutely no one in whose hands the striper should want to be more than Billy's. Time after time I have seen his thumb and forefinger clamped on the lower jaw of a cow bass, it's body still suspended in the coolness of the water, while Billy's hand goes down her throat like an endoscope in search of an obstruction. In most cases, before the bass even realizes what has happened, she's swimming back from whence she came, albeit a little confused. And amazingly, most of this "surgery" is bloodless, or nearly so. For the fish, that is, but not for Billy. His hands take hit after hit—and the mementos of battle, etched on them like the primitive tattoos on *Quequeeg's* face, accumulate throughout the season. There are the parallel, symmetrical strakes of raspy upper and lower jaw plates, the puncture wounds of spines and hooks, the cuts and slices of gill covers and line and other abrasive inflammations of unknown piscatorial origin.

Like I said, Billy's hands are a pathetic mess this season. But don't pity the guy too long. All that really means is that the fishing has rarely been better.

The Paradox

WE'RE AT THE HEIGHT OF THE BASS SEASON and I'm facing a real dilemma: Billy has me sworn to secrecy. Secrecy about everything. About him (which isn't all that much of a challenge), about his boat, about his bait, his methods, his tackle—the whole package of weird idiosyncracies that comprise his fanatical world of fishing. But most of all, Billy has me sworn to secrecy about his fish—which I have started to think of, in some egotistical contortion of reality, as **our** fish.

The closest thing that I can think of to being taken into Billy's fishing confidence would be something like working as a mob prosecutor who has exclusive access to a guy like *Donny Brasco*. If word of the exchange of information ever got out, the golden goose would soon be dead, and there would be a good chance that you wouldn't be feeling too well yourself. Perhaps I exaggerate, but you get the idea. I mean, a few seasons back Billy spent forty-eight hundred of his own hard-earned dollars to repaint the perfectly maintained hull of his boat a different color, just to throw the competition off for a season or two before they'd realize it was still him. Talk about "When the going gets tough…"

So I'm not sure that I can do what Billy wants, and Billy knows it.

We get back to his boat slip one mid-September morning about 11:00 after fishing a lousy tide in the bay. Still, we have caught a shit-load of nice bass, one of which I want to keep to eat. I also watched about a dozen other good fish swim off after being released that trip – and that's a real good feeling too, so I don't feel all that guilty.

"You really want to keep this fish? I mean, it's not exactly a monster."

"Billy, you know Rosalie and I like fish. I spend twenty dollars every time I go to the freaking boutique fish market by my house. Striped bass, when you can get it, goes for ten bucks a pound. Yeah, I'd like to keep that fish, your lordship."

But there's another "fisherman" puttering around his boat as we shoehorn into the pathetic wading pool of a slip where Ms.Nameless spends her leisure time and *The Greek* is not about to flash this twenty-five pounder under this guy's inquiring nose.

"How'd you guys do out there?"

Billy shrugs and says nothing. Me? I've got the routine down pretty well by now:

"We didn't. What about you?"

"They never even touched my eel. I drifted the whole area from the inlet to the lighthouse and never even got a tap. Party boats get nice fish there all the time. I don't get it. Maybe we should save our gas and bait and fish with them, instead."

I hear Billy's brain working, deep within the recesses of what little gray matter there may exist, "I wonder whether this *meatball* spends all his time with his friends 'spaghetti' and 'marinara sauce,' or whether he just lies around in the plate all by himself."

Either way, I decide to head home, *sans* striper, which Billy promises to drop off to me at his earliest opportunity. Something must have come up because I never did get to sample my best recipes on that particular bass.

There is no longer any doubt that I must learn to deal with the paradox of always appearing to fail—if my true desire is to learn how to succeed beyond the level of what most everyone else would consider possible. Even though I am not really a fanatical fisherman, I think that I can be true to the fellowship of the fish. But I know it's not going to be easy.

FRIENDS HAVE STARTED calling me to go out with them.
Guys with real nice boats and great electronics. Guys who
think that because it's the fall and the bass are supposed to be
suicidal nothing can stand in the way of their being able to
catch them too. All they need is a smidgen of insider information and the *bull*—no, I guess I mean the *cow*, market will lay
itself open to their assaults. They roll out of bed in these glo-
rious days of Indian Summer and, emboldened by the residual
warmth of sun on their faces, decide that the time is perfect to
hunt the noble striped denizens of the cooling bay waters.

"I hear they're killing themselves on clam bellies (...or
on live eels—or on bunker—or *Bass Assassins*....) Mike, why
don't you and me go out and get some of these monsters?"

"I hear they're at the bridge (...or at the rip—or at the
Coast Guard Station—or the Lighthouse....)"
"The bite's on the outgoing (or on the incoming—or
high water slack). Where? How? When? Why? And in what
combination?"

In case you haven't figured it out yet, you've entered the
confraternity of more questions than answers.

I walk into **Causeway Bait and Tackle Shop**, located on the
mainland, but not more than a few miles from locations in
the bay where Billy and I have demolished the bass on
numerous occasions. It's an inviting, old-fashioned, tradi-
tional and independent establishment, packed with carefully
selected equipment and staffed by expert owner/advisors.

It's the kind of place where real local knowledge is shared by those who have paid their dues, yet free and useful advice is still disseminated to those who never have, but ask anyway. It's the kind of shop that supplements its regular business by folks who'd ordinarily track down the absolute discount at a mega-store but who realize that when it comes to a fleeting opportunity with the wiley striper, local expertise may be worth the price of admission to the land of the real deal.

So it's one-thirty in the afternoon and the place is jammed. You have to actually wait on line to pay. A young, business-suited woman wants a "landing net" for her husband for his birthday. She is shown a nice item for twenty bucks.

"No, that can't be very good, plus I don't think it's big enough. What about the black one up there?"

"Well, that's really a professional net—it goes for eighty dollars."

"That's fine. Can my husband land a bass with that?"

"Sure. Keep the receipt, though, just in case it's not what he wanted."

Everyone's has striper mania. They want magical fresh bunker to charm big cows to their final destiny, irresistible live eels to lure them to their doom. They want bass from boats drifting lazily on gentle currents during warm, week-end afternoons, bass for their children from the reassuring stability of the *Jones Beach Piers*, bass from the slowly-cooling waters of the gentle ocean surf.

A regular sidles up to the counter. "A pint of fiddlers."

"Still sticking with those little blackfish at the Meadowbrook, Al?"

This exchange goes over the heads of all the early-afternoon crew, but the rest of us just smile.

The rush slows and talk turns to some of the actual fish that have been weighed in during the last few days. A *thirty-nine and a half* (pounds, not inches, I silently hope). A *twenty-seven*. A *thirty-two*. This is killing me. Billy and I just had a *forty-two* and a *forty-five* on the beach two nights ago. We had seventeen fish over twenty from the boat the next day, all released. I have evidence, hard proof, pictures, even video tape.

A middle-aged guy, clearly unknown to the regular crew stumbles into the shop asking if they have a certified scale he can weigh his fish on. He pulls a nice bass out of a huge *Igloo* in the back of his new Ford four by four and drags it to a place of honor located in the official weigh-in area where both he and the shop's name will be recorded for posterity. The needle of the scale strains to twenty-four pounds, six ounces. Only the fisherman's pride appears weightier than his catch. It's his third keeper of the season, caught from his new twenty-seven foot *Aquasport* exactly where his other fish were hooked and landed. It seems that he got it on the first hour of outgoing tide drifting a live bunker past the fourth abutment on the southeast side of the third *Wantagh*.

"Same tidal stage, same wind as all my really good fish, southwest at about ten to fifteen. Give me live bunker near the third Wantagh any time. They're deadly. By the way, when do you think they'll put that picture in *The Fisherman?*"

Rest easy *BTG,* I'm Sicilian. You know I take my blood oaths seriously.

Good News/Bad News

OVER THE YEARS I'VE LEARNED A LOT about fishing from a lot of different people. I've learned from guys who are experts and from guys who are idiots. The idiots teach you what not to do, which is sometimes just as important as learning what works. Just think about the guys who do the same wrong thing, even the same dumb things, over and over again. They fish in the wrong spots, with the wrong baits, during the wrong tides. They might as well be fishing in a swimming pool. Yet they take cast after cast, sometimes for hours, and leave with the distinct impression that there just weren't any fish around. The simple truth of the matter is that there are always some fish around, **somewhere**, almost all of the time. The challenge is that there are many variables that determine if you are going to catch them. And it is never enough to be right with just one or two of these factors. They are all interrelated and must come into alignment together. Think of a slot machine. I've watched players get all excited when they see three red sevens appear in the glass, but not on the pay line. They're pissed because they 'almost hit the jackpot.' Come on, folks, you're still a loser. You've got to line up all the pieces to win. He who can get all his ducks in a row more consistently than the next guy will catch fish more consistently. If you get so good that the whole thing gets to be second nature, you will probably catch fish most of the time. And when I say 'fish,' I always mean striped bass.

Are there fishermen who can do this all the time, or at least almost all the time? You bet your ass there are. Me, for instance.

I talk about catching three, four, five thousand bass a season, sometimes more (don't get excited, in my old age I release practically every one). I know that most people would say that I'm clearly full of shit. That's because they simply can't comprehend my intensity. I fish every single day during the season, and twenty-four hour sessions aren't that uncommon. And, please, allow me to clear up what I mean by a 'twenty-four hour session.' That **doesn't** mean that I sit on one piece all day and night for twenty-four hours straight. It **does** mean that I only spend my time where and when it is likely to be productive. We all know that some tides produce more than others under a certain set of conditions (remember, 'lining up the 7's'). So why the hell would anyone want to waste his time trying to hook bass during a tide that has totally died, or on a beach where the wind has pushed the bait so far offshore that the poor slob casting to them can't come to within seventy-five yards of where the fish are feeding? It's really not rocket science, but it does take experience and fundamental understanding, which almost anyone who is willing to put in the time can learn. I mean, if you want to spend hours planted in a spot under unfavorable conditions that are practically guaranteed to be fishless, hey, go ahead and knock yourself out. The water is pretty, there are lots of nice seagulls, and you'll probably get to see some beautiful sunsets. I want to catch fish, especially real big fish, so I spend my valuable time where there is a good chance that they can be caught using the right techniques.

How it works is simple. If I start fishing a real productive tide in the Jones Inlet area and the fishing goes dead (or never turned on in the first place) I can be at the third *Wantagh* in ten minutes, which will still give me an hour and a half of prime, fast-moving water to fish. If you really learn the in's and out's of a specific area of water you can actually fish eight, ten—even a dozen locations that are only minutes apart—where the tide conditions will be dramatically different and much more conducive to catching fish. Remember, though, conditions are also going to change according to winds, bait and lunar cycles. You can **start** with a set of tide tables, but anyone who is going to be a consistent producer has to do his own homework and tweak the stuff that is available to the general public. That takes time and effort. That's what is meant by 'paying your dues.'

Going back to the '24/7' concept, let me give just one example. During a tremendous fall bite a few seasons back I took my buddy Jeff Morales out on a trip. Jeff is a good fisherman who can really push the limits when he smells action. We started off in the vicinity of the *Fire Island Light* and then traveled to the *Meadowbrook* region for a few hours. When conditions deteriorated, I headed west to *Atlantic Beach*. On the way back we covered some of the same spots, again under prime tide conditions, as we worked our way east. On that particular trip Jeff met me at the boat at 5:00 a.m. and I had my first fish on before six. We got back to my dock at 7:30 the following morning. I won't tell you exactly how many fish we caught that day because you won't believe me anyway. But Jeff can attest to the fact that we had thirty-seven fish before we left our first spot. Now here's the real amazing part that I hope you **do** believe because it will give you an idea of what someone has to be prepared to do to put up impressive numbers in hope of getting to real good fish. We left the dock that morning with one hundred beautiful fresh bunker—packed in **saltwater** ice in two 150 gallon *Igloos*—and a hundred gallons of gas. That's for a skiff with a big outboard, not a thirty-one foot, twin screw sportsfisherman. We also had a few thermoses of coffee, a couple of heroes from my friend's deli and a bag of *Ring-Dings*. Now I ask you, who else do you know who would invest all that money in chocolate-covered little round cakes?

Kidding aside, what I'm describing is not unusual for my trips. I mean, I'm not going to break the bank when I suspect that the pickings will be slim, but I do have the absolute confidence in my own ability to go out fully prepared to locate fish and catch them in large numbers. Remember, I'm looking for really big fish. The reality of this kind of fishing is that you will wade through a lot of twenty and thirty pounders while looking for the sixty or (please, God) seventy pound monster. So what good could it possibly do to locate a huge school of big bass that manage to eat up your pathetic six baits before you hook your first few fish? And what if you find out that the bite is torrid at the next inlet over when your gas gauge is pushing empty and the sun is going down?

If I'm fishing dead bunker, I don't leave the dock with less than fifty prime baits. I'd rather throw them to the crabs and seagulls than find myself short during a blitz. Plus I go through a thousand pounds of **saltwater** ice a week when bait fishing—and three hundred-fifty to five hundred dollars worth of gas. P.S. If you're going to hold fresh bunker on ice cubes from the fridge or let them float belly-up in a luke-warm bait-well during a trip—don't expect to hook a lot of bass—unless they're the dumb and starving variety—or they show a distinct preference for bouillabaisse. And before you get the impression that I'm some kind of millionaire, let me set the money piece straight. I'm lucky enough to be the owner/operator of my own business and earn a pretty good living on my own terms, making my own hours. Most of my work is done during the off-season or during down-times in the fishing. Anyone who knows me, though, knows that striped bass come first. If the choice is between scheduling a profitable job versus nailing some huge bass, you better believe that the job will be put on hold.

Yes, I am married and have two teenage kids. I don't think that Dee, my wife, ever really believed what my priorities actually were before we were married—even though she personally witnessed my obsession with fishing. But she definitely understands now, and my family works around my insane schedule.

The last big piece for now concerns my superior skills in bartering. I mean, if I had to pay cold cash for all my fishing-related activities and supplies I would have been in debtor's prison a long time ago. I don't have any connections for gas, so three hundred-fifty to five hundred bucks a week comes out of my pocket. I don't sell fish, so I just have to work a little harder at my business to feed the big Merc. The rest, thank God, comes from my 'benefactors.' It seems that the combination of my specialized knowledge of bass matched with my irresistible personal charm never fails to get me what I need. In the inner circles, I always acknowledge the superiority of the tackle that I use and steer the serious guys to the best sources of quality bait and equipment. Most bait and tackle shops are owned by serious fishermen. They appreciate serious advice.

Still, I can practically hear the brains working out there as I speak:

'The math is still impossible. That would be anywhere between ten and twenty striped bass a day, each and every day of a two hundred-fifty day striped bass season. Yeah, right! Maybe for a haul-seiner or a gill-netter, but no way for a non-commercial fisherman!'

Sorry guys, the numbers **are** right, and the numbers **do** add up. The problem with most would-be fisherman is that they simply don't have the time or the resources or the compulsion to do what I do. Most people still retain some degree of sanity. So they look for shortcuts, or they satisfy themselves with the six-keeper season. That's fine—because then you don't have to play by big league rules. Fact is, the rules can be learned by almost anyone—but applying them with consistency—that's another installment in the saga."

TOBAY WAS A broken picket fence of surfcasters hurling their offerings into the darkening sea. It was late October. Word was out that the bite was on.

When conditions seemed right (which was several hours after what the horde of fishless casters already on the beach seemed to think) *The Greek* surveyed the least conspicuous route to the area where he sensed that the fish would show up on this night. It was obviously not to be in the same area where he had caught five fish to forty-two pounds the night before, because he trudged right past the cadre of wannabe's that had staked out their claim to that particular piece of real estate long before sunset. But Billy did not ignore them just because he was antisocial. No, he knew that conditions had changed significantly over the past twenty-four hours. His extrapolation of relevant factors now placed the site of potential action considerably farther to the west. Consciously avoiding the shoreline, he labored through the tough, deep sands of the higher beach until he disappeared into the dense cover of night. Once out of sight, he moved toward the surf line. In spite of all his attempts at stealth, however, he still found himself being greeted by a familiar voice. The words were the words of Stevie Hollywood and they paid Billy one of the highest compliments he had ever received:

"*Greek,* thank God! When no one saw you we figured the action might be over. Everyone knows that when *The Greek* shows up, the fish gotta be here."

Stevie Hollywood pictured with **BTG** following an outing to remember. These fish are both not very far from the magical **60** pound mark! What more can you say?

Imitation may really be the sincerest form of flattery because a lot of guys follow Billy's example with embarrassing consistency. Let's face it, *Tobay Beach* didn't look like a hot day in mid-August that cold and windy October evening just because a bunch of eager beavers decided to cold-canvass the angry surf line on **their** gut feelings alone. No, *The Greek* had nailed some very nice fish the night before and he knew that the eyes he felt at his back didn't belong to one of the local red foxes that sometimes stalked the dune grasses after sunset.

"It's amazing how most guys can't keep information to themselves, even if it eventually kills their own game to share it. And the real kick in the head is that some of these *meatballs* don't even need to actually catch fish to experience a sense of accomplishment. Just reporting to someone else that they were an eyewitness to an impressive catch makes them feel like superstars. I mean, calling in close friends and fishing partners—that's one thing—but total strangers? Just to be the hero who broke the news? Give me a freaking break!

The bottom line is all about developing confidence and gaining independence. A lot of guys are perfectly happy to play follow the leader—waiting around until someone else locates the fish and specifies the techniques for catching them. That's why good party boats are always surrounded by mosquito fleets and almost all good fisherman, no matter what their specialty, are stalked like Hollywood movie stars. When I give workshops, I'm not looking to increase the ranks of the followers—I **am** looking to help fishermen begin to understand the fundamentals of this art, this science, so well that eventually they won't need anyone to point them in the right direction. They will be able to assess any set of circumstances on their own, make their own decisions—and catch their own fish. As long as your only desire is to get specific information that will put you into fish for a tide, or for a day or for the duration of a bite—your fish-catching will end when those particular circumstances change. Believe me, when a guy like Stevie Hollywood equates my presence with the presence of striped bass, that goes a long way toward increasing my hat size. But you noticed, I hope, that on the particular night I spoke about, Stevie was already in the spot that I was heading for. That's because Stevie has learned to read the page and comprehend its meaning.

Once you get to understand what this game is really all about, you get to know what to do all the time. When that happens, you make your own specifics. You make your own luck. **That's** what it's all about. **That's** the only point I really need for you to get."

The Learning Curve

THERE ARE MANY TIMES when I go out without any intention of actually catching fish. Those days and nights are investments in the future. In my opinion, they are the most valuable hours that you can put in. Those are the trips that teach you how to think like a fish. Once you start thinking like a fish, you're pretty much set for life. If you're not willing to spend a lot of time on research, though, you're never going to be able to think on your own feet. You're always going to want someone to give you the specifics. You'll never get to the theory behind the circumstances that always produce fish.

A good part of this game has to do with developing confidence in your own abilities. I swear that I've been out hundreds of times with guys who are supposed to be real good fishermen when all they do is prepare you for failure. And the style of fishing doesn't matter. They'll tell you on the ride to the beach, or on the ride to their favorite piece of bottom—whatever—that 'conditions may not be right today' or 'the bait patterns may have changed' or 'the main body of the school may have moved to another location.' Talk about insecurity. Give me a freaking break. When guys talk like this it always means one of three things to me. Either the guy isn't any good to begin with, or he is, but doesn't want to give away his hand, or he just doesn't have a very high level of confidence in his own abilities and wants you to know that if the fish don't bite on this particular trip, you shouldn't really blame him. That's usually the main reason.

If you remember the great old movie version of *Moby Dick* with Gregory Peck, think about the scene when *Starbuck* comes down into the captain's cabin as Ahab, looking all crazed and obsessed, pours over his secret chart of the movements of whales. No GPS, no Loran, no depth recorders, no nothing–yet the captain has pinpointed where and when the giants can be intercepted throughout the oceans of the world. His first mate is stunned at Ahab's incredible calculations and astounded by his amazing perceptions. The old master doesn't need to follow any fleet— he makes his own success.

I have done my homework for over thirty-five years. I don't need anyone to tell me where they think the fish may be or why. Or, for that matter, why not. Whenever I go out, I go out with the absolute expectation of catching fish. I know that I won't annihilate them every time, that much I accept, but neither will I make excuses ahead of time as to why the fishing may not be good. That's why I always go out loaded for bear whenever I intend to fish. What the hell is the sense of going bait fishing with two or three fresh bunker or half a dozen live eels. Lose a few baits to the bottom or to hungry bluefish and you're out of business for the trip. All that says to me is that you don't intend to be successful.

Now I don't want you to get the totally wrong impression. You may be thinking to yourself that you don't just happen to have a spare lifetime or two to develop the uncanny abilities required to play in this kind of league. Well, the truth of the matter is that there aren't that many absolute fundamentals to learn. If you're willing to listen and learn them the **right** way, though—you'll be well on your way to becoming an independent, consistent producer of striped bass, including some of the big boys."

Here's what I'm talking about.

THE STORIES HAVE a thousand variations, but the common thread is always the same: specific knowledge works for specific situations; fundamental knowledge can be adapted to work for any situation. Pick a specialty and apply the rule—it always holds true. *Ergo,* you have to "teach a man to fish…"

Billy concerns himself with all the essentials of salt water fishing in their most elemental form and customizes their application as needed. The good news is that there really aren't that many essentials to learn.

"If you're pinning me down on specifics, you're in luck because there won't be all that much to write—but starting to understand the real deal—that's another story.

First of all everyone out there has to know that I am talking about fishing for very large striped bass in local salt waters. I am not dealing with Hudson River bass (which play a major role in the equation, but aren't targeted much by Long Island bass fishermen) or hybrid bass that have been introduced into fresh water environments for various reasons. I am talking strictly about techniques for salt water fishing in any area that is affected by tidal flow. Why this is critical will be explained later. On Long Island, that would include the bays, the ocean beaches and inshore ocean grounds, the north shore harbors and the *Sound,* itself. Naturally, it would also include any bodies of salt water with similar characteristics—and that includes a tremendous number of fishable areas in the Northeast and even quite a few West Coast locations. Which brings up the first absolutely essential point.

Specialize

By this I simply mean that you really have no choice but to limit the area where you intend to fish.

If you're fishing for reasons other than mine (which is to catch the biggest possible striped bass with the most consistency—even when everyone else is grumbling that such fish no longer exist) then you can disregard this suggestion. Your priorities might include expanding your travel horizons, birdwatching or even discovering the most beautiful locations for spectacular sunsets—but they shouldn't include an expectation to consistently catch really big striped bass. It's not that many, many areas don't hold big fish, it's that you can't possibly learn the most important factors that are essential to know in order to catch them all the time. Not in one lifetime, not in two or three. And that's coming from a guy who spends over *eighteen hundred hours* on or at the water each and every year. Please notice how often I refer to the idea of consistency. It should be understood that when I talk about talented or successful fishermen, I am talking about guys who produce fish nearly all the time, trip after trip, season after season. Anybody is capable of stumbling into a good fish at any time by total surprise or total coincidence.

Think of party boat trips where a first-time kid lands the pool fish—or the guy who drags a forty pound bass that he hooked on a flounder rig into a local tackle shop. No, if a guy is to be respected as a real fisherman, he has to be capable of producing under virtually any conditions—not always with the same degree of success, but with **some** degree of success, ninety to ninety-five percent of the time. My own personal rule is that I won't go home until I've caught at least one fish. *Sometimes that means I don't get to go home when I planned to.* But back to the main point.

If you want to develop consistency you must get to the point that when you go out under a given set of conditions you know your area so well that you are absolutely confident that you are going to get fish. Confidence is an intangible but highly significant factor—and you will never develop real confidence if you keep running around from area to area trying to chase the movement of the fish that you either heard about at the local watering hole or read about in the local magazines. This is true of any method of fishing, but it is critical when it comes to trailering a boat. If you think that you can launch your center-console in a totally unfamiliar area and proceed to do a job on highly selective, fabulously-instinctive fish like big striped bass—then you've been sniffing too much of your guide-wrapping cement during the off season. This doesn't mean that you can't or shouldn't make exploratory trips. It simply means that you must learn to specialize in a delimited area where you know everything about the region that you elect to concentrate your efforts in. That's where you should make your exploratory trips, in fact. I spend ninety percent of my time in a cross section of the *Island* not much more than fifteen miles long and two miles wide. I believe that I know as much as anyone possibly can know about that area of submerged real estate. There are literally thousands of boats—private, recreational and commercial—that fish that area for two-thirds of the year, year in and year out. I know that I catch more striped bass than any of these guys and that no one comes close to the total numbers of big fish that I land and release every season. Not necessarily the biggest single fish, mind you, but the most big fish over the long haul. I do this because I know the area cold. I make it my business to monitor every parameter that affects how big stripers behave in those regions that I share with them. I monitor how conditions change from day to day. I know the variation in current strength from one marsh bank to another only a hundred yards away. It's simply impossible for anyone to be that knowledgeable, that intimate, about every area that holds fish. Impossible. So that's the first commitment you must make if you want to succeed. Learn a limited area—and learn it cold."

Tide and Current

I MADE THE INITIAL POINT ABOUT STRIPED BASS in salt water because those are the waters that are influenced by tidal conditions. If you're fishing land-locked lakes, you still have to learn all you can about conditions that affect the fishing in order to be successful, but tide is not one of them.

In salt water fishing, tide is the make or break consideration—but one that seems to remain a deep mystery, even to fishermen who otherwise know their stuff. I will not go into all the astronomical factors that affect the tides right now but will insist that you must develop an accurate understanding of tide and current flow in order to consistently catch striped bass. The problem is that most fishermen are clueless about tide, and even those who think they know, really don't.

Bass have to eat. Big bass have to eat a lot. But big bass like to inhale their prey with the least effort possible. More than any other factor in fishing, it is *tide* and *current* that determine when and how big bass will be able to accomplish this, their primary objective in life. Bass, often more than other fish, will bite best on certain stages of the tide in certain areas and under certain conditions. Those factors are the specifics that you must learn and the reason why I insist that you must limit your most intensive efforts to a given area. But it still does no good to know that the bite has been hottest at *Gilgo* on the first hour of the falling tide with a light south-west breeze during the daylight hours—if you don't really know what actual time of day those exact tidal conditions will occur.

'But I study the tide tables and follow them exactly for my area,' you protest.

Let me ask you this. How many times have you studied those tables, arrived at the given spot at the 'perfect' time for the optimal tidal conditions and found that the tide isn't doing what it's supposed to be doing . What you really mean, of course is that it's not doing what you expected it to be doing! **If that's happened to you more than once, that's too many times!** Sometimes, you won't even know that something is wrong. On the beach, for instance. If you're boat fishing in the bay and there are many nearby reference points to help you evaluate the tidal stage—pilings, bridge abutments, whatever—at least you'll be able to visually **observe** that you've made a boo-boo. At the surf line, however, an hour error in assessing tidal stage doesn't carry any obvious visual markers—other than the absence of the fish that were supposed to be blitzing the beach—or the total disappearance of good fishermen who had the proper understanding of tidal stages and currents. While you're fishing what you think was the first hour of the outgoing, along with the other *meatballs* who thought the same, I'm catching fish at a location where the conditions are appropriate—or spending my time more productively over eggs and homefries at the nearest twenty-four hour diner.

If you don't understand tides and currents and the specifics of how they behave in your area, then you cannot catch fish consistently—especially really big fish. I've actually heard guys insist that 'the tide is wrong.' Hello! The tide is never wrong. The tide is always right for any set of conditions at a given place and at a given point in time. No, it's not the tide that's wrong, it's you who are wrong. If you're not willing to learn why, you might as well hang it up.

So before you even think about anything else, start off by learning the difference between *tide* and *current*.

Tide is the vertical rise and fall of the water. **Current** is the horizontal movement of the same.

If you arrive at a bridge in your boat to clam chum bass on the first of the outgoing water and hit the location at exactly the time when the newspaper tables indicated 'high tide,' you will quickly discover that the *tide* **is** as high as it's going to get, but that the *current* is still flowing **in** and will be doing so for quite some time. You will, in fact, have to wait anywhere from an hour and a half up to three full hours before conditions become what you expected them to be upon your arrival. That is why you must look at 'high water slack' specifications for the area where you intend to fish, not merely at 'high tide' tables. But it doesn't end there. You must understand that published *tide* and *current* tables are very general in the data they provide. If you ever want to become a true expert you must refine and customize the information they present so that you know exactly what the water movement will be for the specific locations that you intend to fish. Only then will you be able to develop a specialized bag of tricks that will enable you to fish productively and efficiently while ninety-five percent of the other guys just sit and hope that a particularly stupid fish will want to commit suicide just at the moment when their bait is in the water.

If you follow my advice and really learn an area with a depth of knowledge that far exceeds the hordes of casual fishermen out there, do not make the fatal mistake of neglecting to keep a written record of the invaluable information that you have gathered. Write down everything you learn—and do it as soon as possible after you experience it. If you wait too long, your recollection of specifics will be clouded. If you are religious in your attention to the recording of these essential details, it won't be long before you know nuances of tide, current, wind, bait, tackle and presentation differentials that put you into fish and the 'competition' into a state of total frustration.

How important are the minute details? Friends who know me know that I'm a loner. I hope by now I've established the point as to why secretiveness has to be part of the game. Many times when a crowd gathers I will move. Sometimes, however, I will continue to fish—surrounded by boats in the bay or by casters at the surf line. The difference between us? I'm devastating the fish and they're pulling their hair out. I have to admit that I get a real kick out of that scenario sometimes. Why does it occur? Again, it's all in the details. It's usually nothing more than something as miniscule as a split shot to adjust for current strength, or an extra sixteen inches of leader length that alters the flutter of a bait, or the angle that I cut my bunker chunks on. Subtleties like these, though are easily correctable. But believe me, if you're not catching fish because you think that you're fishing an outgoing tide when in reality the current is still roaring into the bay, then you have a real problem. Then you have to go back to the basics and start your study of this game all over again. But for now, start with the naked essentials:

Tides and currents control the movement and vulnerability of bait.

Big bass require a considerable amount of nourishment, which they prefer to acquire with the smallest possible expenditure of energy.

Learn the tidal stages and current movements that produce the most favorable feeding conditions for big stripers and you will position yourself to catch them with consistency."

SEVERAL YEARS BACK, long after the fabulous early '70's run of local weakfish in the *Fire Island* area had ended, Billy showed me how to catch the giant *tiderunners* that still hung out in the region, unbeknownst to anyone else. This was strictly a night fishery and with the coming of dawn one morning *The Greek* suggested that we move across to the ocean side to fish for blues with the bait we still had left. A run of big bluefish had been on for a few days and Billy knew that I'd get a kick out of catching these bruisers in the suds at *Jones Beach*. When we arrived at the water the surf line was already well-populated with casters fishing bait from sand-spiked rods. There were no fish in evidence nor were there any of the usual signs of their immediate presence.

Billy set up in characteristic silence, avoiding communication with anyone else but me. It was September and most of the other guys were in waders and full surf outfits. We were in jeans and sneakers.We employed totally conventional "fish-finder" rigs baited with fresh bunker slabs, but without wire leaders. Within minutes we were both into fish—big teen sized, mongo bluefish. They bent our rods over sharply and fought like little trucks. We landed both fish—Billy's long before mine—and quickly proceeded to release them into the gently-rolling surf.

Many eyes turned to us.

Back in the water, two more fish. Release them. Bait up. Repeat. More eyes.

Billy doesn't eat fish and I don't really love the oily-flavored dark shards of mature bluefish myself, so each fighting loco-motive, even if somewhat bloodied, went back into his domain as gently as possible.

We broke off a few fish. Onlookers were quick to point out that they were lost to the absence of wire leaders, which we had foolishly failed to employ, as required, in **our** blue-fish rigs.

They were probably right.

Just before we were getting ready to leave, a very frustrated-looking middle-aged gentleman accosted Billy:

"If you don't want those damn fish, why don't you give them to me—I like to eat them."

Billy, just in the process of unhooking another bruiser leaned to the water line and guided the blue to freedom. He turned his head toward this poor, frustrated old soul:

"Here, why don't you catch this one—he's seems stupid enough to bite again—even on a proper bluefish rig with a wire leader and all."

Then the bluefish kicked his tail fin into high gear and head-ed for points south and west.

That night my wife and I barbecued a big weakfish on a hibachi in the courtyard of our garden apartment. The fish was so big that we decided to invite four of our friends over to join us. Delicious. Much better than the big blues that I knew were on their way to fight another day.

All This And
Philanthropy Too

FAME BY ASSOCIATION is almost always a good thing. I can only see it as bad when the ego boost you derive from dropping a high profile name is overshadowed by envy of whatever it is that has made an individual so highly recognized in the first place.

The latter circumstance was never my problem with Billy. I was never jealous that he caught so many fish—because he was, after all, crazy. I mean, who in his right mind would choose to sacrifice so many of life's amenities just to pursue fish? Still, I welcomed any opportunity to lay claim to a personal association with Billy because I fished quite a bit myself and I figured that it could only bolster my own reputation to be known as a confidante and sometime partner of the legendary *Greek*. I was to learn that such was not always to be the case.

In the very early days, back in the late '60's, Billy was nothing more than a wisecracking kid who caught an unbelievable number of large striped bass. But in that decade and the one to follow, so did almost everyone else. Even rank amateurs took ten to twenty fish a trip—many more if clam-chumming school fish, generally less if bunker-dunking big cows along the ocean jetties. Although the catches would be embarrassing by today's standards of conservation-driven fishing ethics, they were very much legal then. Even though the kill rate was astounding, almost no one believed that what they were doing was contributing to the total decimation of the striped bass fishery.

IN THOSE DAYS Billy sold his fish, something he needed to do to defray expenses, but something that didn't endear him to the hearts of many sportsfishermen. Not that they wouldn't be more than willing to accept his tips on where, when and how if he were ever willing to share his expertise. But he wasn't. So the reputation he earned was that of a "meat" fisherman who didn't always play by the rules of fishing etiquette. Rumors of hundred pound test line and rods built like telephone poles began to circulate. Some even insisted that Billy had to be netting his fish. Truth is, the average fisherman, totally incapable of coming within a nautical mile of matching Billy's numbers, had to suggest some type of foul play to explain *The Greek's* incredible scores and his even more incredible consistency. Even after the bubble burst and the fish seemed to vanish for almost everyone else, Billy was still catching big bass, and in numbers that hadn't diminished very much. This was not a scenario that led to the veneration of *The Greek* as a folk hero. But I didn't really consider the "greening" of fishermen's emotions and how that phenomenon affects the perception of reputations. I still pursued almost every opportunity to recount the accomplishments of **my** friend, Billy Legakis, but was occasionally set back by some of the assessments that were proffered in regard to a side of *The Greek* that I hadn't known. So for every guy who described Billy as "the best striped bass fisherman on Long Island," or "the best striped bass fisherman I have ever known," it was not uncommon to come across others who said that he compulsively lied about his catches, employed unethical fishing techniques, was a real "low-life bastard," or was generally "full of shit." On more than one occasion it was suggested to me that *The Greek* was actually all of the above.

Two *Fifty Plus* fish out of the four landed that night.

NOW I'VE KNOWN for some time that *The Greek's* engaging personality traits sometimes prevent him from becoming everyone's best friend. He's never been shy about articulating "constructive" criticism that he observes in the methods of others, and he does have a most endearing way of deflating the egos of guys who think that their twenty-five pounder is the fish of a lifetime. When questioned, in fact, about the "unsportsmanlike" heft of the tackle that he regularly employs, Billy unabashedly responds that he uses it for the express purpose of wading through just such unremarkable fish quickly—in hope of "getting to the cows that often hang around with these little 'rats'." Billy doesn't have much patience for incompetence—and you have no chance of walking the same sand with him if he suspects that you might value something else in life more than catching monster striped bass. Every once in a while it's true that Billy will alter his style to humor a guy like me, modifying the intensity of a trip to less demanding parameters than he sets for himself. But even I was given no choice on a boat trip that was scheduled to last "only until the first half of the outgoing" when the bite didn't start until the first half of the incoming tide. I would really have enjoyed the sunrise that I got unexpectedly to see that morning, too, if I didn't have to be at work within an hour of our eventual arrival at the dock.

Yet extraordinary circumstances for other serious anglers sometime elicit almost philanthropic responses from Billy.

Several seasons back, *Greek* was doing his late fall thing from the top of a bridge near *Jones Inlet*. Conditions were cold and breezy, leaving the structure deserted in the middle of this late November night. Most striper fishermen had already stored their equipment away for the year. But these were the days that Billy lived for—the "miss it if you blink" season of *late cruisers* that hung around until the bitter end, greedily picking off the fat herring that were drawn into the light display of the bridges. Billy loved the isolation of these conditions, the ability to focus exclusively on the fish, the total absence of prying eyes. Hazy outlines of jet black velveteen shapes hung motionless just below the surface of the rushing waters. Few fishermen would know what they represented even if they had the ability to perceive them, but Billy needed no further evidence that he was once again in the right place at the right time. Each cast produced a fish, but not just any fish. These bass were all monsters, each one could easily be considered the fish of someone else's lifetime. From the first moment he arrived, Billy knew that this was to be no ordinary night.

The Greek had already landed two magnificent fish, both weighing over fifty pounds and was working on a third good bass when he recognized the silhouette of a familiar figure. Far to his right, toward the northern end of the span, Tony Iszu was struggling against the brute force of what appeared to be a very powerful bass. It was the same Tony who had encountered Billy on the bridge two years earlier. Billy was stalking the span, scoping out the waters for signs of big stripers. He spotted the outline of a huge fish, but it was Tony, not him, who occupied the walkway just above the shadow line where the monster bass had taken up residence. This posed somewhat of a dilemma.

"Believe it or not, there aren't many guys who pursue this highly specialized style of bass fishing from the bridges in the late fall. You will come across all kinds of *meatballs* fishing the bridges at night in the spring and summer when the weather is nice, but there aren't too many maniacs like me who are willing to make the sacrifices that it takes to practice this technique as November is coming to a close. I knew Tony as a serious surf fisherman who had paid his dues. If he was willing to tough out a night hunting the big boys, who was I to bitch about it?

So here was Tony Iszu, standing right over a bass that had to go well over forty. The fish was at his feet, straight down twenty-seven feet below the bridge deck where he was standing. Like most big bass on bridges at this time of year, this cow was right below the surface of the water, motionless. All the conditions were perfect. I stared at the huge outline of the monster, then back at Tony who greeted me with a big hello. Fact is, the unwritten etiquette of die-hard bridge fishermen dictated that Tony had first dibs on that fish. But Tony was acting like I was the only sign of life in the area. The fish hadn't moved, but, amazingly, neither had Tony. He started up a conversation with me as if the huge fish hadn't existed."

"Yeah, nice seeing you too, Tony, but why the hell don't you cast to that fish?"

"I haven't gotten a bump since I got here over an hour ago, *Greek*. Doesn't look like we're going to get nothing tonight. What fish are you talking about?"

"Tony, there's a giant fish right below you—clear as day, just sitting there waiting to be caught. Don't you see him? He's right there!"

"*Greek*," I don't see nothing. Let me tell you, nobody I ever fished with has eyes like you. I know you better, though, than to say you're seeing things, so go ahead, you take a cast."

164 • Michael G. Cinquemani

"Having fulfilled my moral responsibility, I did, and proceeded to instantaneously hook a bass that later weighed in at just over forty-six pounds. I can never understand how other guys miss seeing fish like these, but they seem to, all the time. Maybe I have some sixth sense about it, or something, but I never miss seeing these fish.

So here we are again, same place, different time, but now Tony has a fish on. It was obviously a good fish, too, but it looked liked Tony was going to have a tough time getting him in. If you're not used to landing big stripers from a bridge that's high off the water, believe me, it can be a humbling experience. Assuming that you've been able to turn the bass and gain good control over him, you then have to work the fish from wherever you hooked him over to the nearest ground that slopes to the shore. This could involve more than a hundred yard walk while tethered to a powerful, still-fighting bass who just might have other plans than you for the night. Naturally, as you move it's necessary to pass your rod around the light poles and other obstructions along the way. Assuming that you've gotten this far, then the fun really begins. This part calls for considerable strength, agility and not a little bit of fancy foot work. Keeping constant tension on the line, you hop down the slope, mountain goat style, reeling in the slack as you go. When you get to the water you simply grab the fish, which should be in the general vicinity of your feet, and hold on for dear life. If you need artificial light to guide you down the slope or to illuminate the fish, you have a problem. If you need a net or a gaff to land the fish, the advantage tilts further in favor of old *roccus*. I never carry any extra gear with me so it's a lot easier for me to get down to the fish. I never have a problem grabbing any size fish by the lower jaw and hanging on to him, come hell or high water. I never drop a fish once I grab him. Never. If you're shy about doing this or don't feel that you have the ability or the strength to do it, then this style of fishing may not be your personal shot of tequila. If you feel that you have to use a hand gaff, remember that's one extra piece of baggage you'll have to carry. You could forget it, lose it or not be able to negotiate the slope because of it. You can't pull the fish out by the leader—because that's asking for trouble. I'd suggest that if you're serious about trying this type of fishing that you learn how to land fish—any size fish—the way I do. You do it just like you see all the freshwater guys doing—grabbing big-mouths by the lower jaw. Just do it with a lot more conviction and tenacity. I'd suggest you start by practicing on every fish you catch—boat-caught, surf-caught, whatever. Once you develop the confidence to do it right, you'll never have to worry about that issue again. Dragging the fish back up the forty-five degree incline is another story, but adrenaline generally helps out by this point. If you're strong and in good shape, you'll be breathing hard—but at least you'll still be breathing. If you're not, a partner who knows CPR might turn out to be your best friend.

So I'm getting a little concerned about Tony and ask if he could use a hand. By this time I've landed my third fish—which, I have trouble believing myself, is another monster over fifty. I mean, **I'm** starting to hyperventilate. And the fish are still there. I can see them as clear as day! But Tony definitely looks like he could use a little help at this point.

Hey, Tony, you want me to go down and get your fish?"

"Yeah, *Greek*, that would be really great if you wouldn't mind."

Moments later, Billy hoisted Iszu's very impressive fish high

enough for him to clearly see what he had hooked. With absolutely no hint of insincerity, sarcasm or facetiousness *The Greek* shouted out,
"Tony, do you want me to keep him for you or let him go?"

It was obvious that Tony felt compelled to replicate some degree of the casual tone of Billy's question with a reply that moderated his sense of total elation with the substantial dimensions of his catch:

"I think I'll keep him, *Greek*. Do you think he'll go fifty?"

Billy responded, "Oh, he's a fifty. Definitely a fifty."

"I passed the fish over to Tony, who was obviously very grateful for my help. He was later to advise me that the bass weighed in at fifty pounds, seven ounces. Tony said it was the best fish he had caught in his entire career—his first long sought after "fifty".

Before I left for the night, I hooked one more striper. *Fifty-two, eleven.* Amazing night, truly amazing. And if I had to share it with anyone, I'm glad it was with a guy like Tony."

Sound too fantastic to believe? Yes, I know, but before you pass judgement, I'd suggest you check with Tony Iszu.

In the meantime, I'll keep my money on *The Greek.*

Genealogy

With a name like *Legakis,* the origin of Billy's moniker should be pretty obvious. But the actual story is worth a slight detour here. Billy didn't actually come to be renamed *"The Greek"* (more accurately articulated without the preposition, as simply *"Greek"*) because of anything related to fishing. If anything competed for Billy's attention in the early days, it was the game of pool and the easy money that attended its skillful practice. Billy began frequenting *The Cue*, a pool hall in Rockville Centre that was owned by Russian immigrants with accents thicker than bunker chum. Seeing that Billy was becoming a regular, one of the owners eventually asked for his name.

"Legakis...Bill Legakis."

The international entrepreneur immediately recognized the national origin of the surname and responded, in a tone always interpreted to be hilarious by all onlookers, "Oh, you're *Grek!*" While good for a couple of laughs at the time, not a whole lot was to become of this baptism until several years later when the story was resurrected amongst a group of Billy's fishing companions. From that point on, anyone who came to know Billy well came to know him as *"Billy the Greek."*

Ocean Cycles

The literature and folklore are filled with stories of the way it used to be. The last old timers still reminisce on outings that today seem fantastic, still recollect with tinges of nostalgic sadness catches that we will never see. Clammers who once supported families with the hard-shelled fruits of the western Great South Bay have themselves become a species more endangered than the bivalves which sustained them. Entire species have been eradicated or reduced to "endangered" status. Some have been gone so long that photographic evidence is all that remains. The lowly *sheepshead*—emblem species that gave the *Bay* its name, can no longer be recalled, its memory having been lost with the passing of the last wizened sea dogs who once stood faithful vigil for head boats returning to their Brooklyn berths.

Whatever ones political affiliations, whatever ones interest in the pursuit of creatures of the sea, no one wanted to see the striped bass end up as just a memory. Once again, *management* was thrust upon the scene and, in the case of *morone saxatilus,* many of the outcomes have proven favorable. A striper "famine" seemed to have been averted, but the balance continues to remain as delicate as any ecological consideration in the affairs of men. Some would insist that a total moratorium is still needed. Most, at the very least, would condemn the excesses of the past.

Billy was born in 1954 and was catching his first striped bass by '66. The glory days were upon us and, as is so often the case in times of plenty, it looked as if those days would never end. There were no size limits, no season closures, no catch restrictions. The striped bass was a highly sought after market fish that always brought in good money. Haul-seining out east and pin-hooking anywhere big schools could be located were the favored commercial methods of catching. For the sportsfisherman, however, stripers still remained one of the greatest challenges to an angler's skill. Guys who could fill their boats with virtually any other species in the neighborhood still had trouble scoring with striped bass with any real consistency. Those who did either contented themselves with life in the shadows, or earned the highly enviable reputation of being known as a striped bass "sharpie." In those days, quite a few fishermen along the northeast coast rose to informal membership in that highly exclusive confraternity. They all paid their dues, fished hard and long under sometimes ugly conditions and managed to rack up big scores of very big fish. By the time he was sixteen, Billy would already have been considered a ranking member of the club had he wanted to join. But he didn't. He knew that he could pay his own way in life with the proceeds of his fanaticism, which is what he elected to do for many years, but he kept his accomplishments largely to himself. In those days he caught, kept and often sold thousands and thousands of striped bass.

"For a while I was totally obsessed with getting bigger and bigger fish. My first decent fish, which I caught when I was thirteen, was a thirty-five pounder. I knew that there were much bigger fish out there because I had seen them with my own eyes. Commercial guys and part-time pinhookers regularly brought in fifty and sixty pound bass that didn't even turn a head with the group I hung out with in those days. Believe me, there were a lot of monster bass and I caught tons of them—sometimes thirty or forty fish over thirty pounds on a single tide. And remember, I wasn't the only guy who was literally slaughtering these humongous stripers.

It wasn't long, though, before I realized that big fish weren't worth a whole lot in the market, so I turned my attention to the much smaller school size bass that were practically worth their weight in gold. Those were the fish that really supported me in the days before I got married, had kids and established my own business."

But that was then.

"For me, those days are gone forever. Not because it's impossible for me to catch numbers or sizes like that again, but because I have developed a dramatically different attitude toward this fish. I will still fish for striped bass with every last bit of energy that I can muster until I can no longer cast a lure—but now I target only the very largest members of the species—and will do everything in my power to preserve the many other fish that I encounter along the way.

I've been called a hypocrite. I've been called much worse. At least let me explain why the first allegation is wrong.

I make no apologies for the fishing excesses of my youth. They were in the past and they served a valid purpose. Still, a day rarely passes that I don't hear comments like 'The *Greek* is nothing but a meat fisherman who uses tackle more like a construction crane than a fishing outfit.'

For years I have been an advocate of beefy rods and high-test line. Everyone who knows me knows that I regularly utilize fifty-pound test conventional tackle under almost all conditions. I do so for one reason. I target big fish. To get to big fish I will often wade through dozens of smaller bass—twenty and thirty pounders. Remember, if you are out for fifty pound plus stripers, even a forty would be considered small. This isn't arrogance, it's just a simple fact. I said before that the old days of loading the boat with fish are gone for me forever, and I mean that. If you would pull up to me in the bay (forget that idea, but if you did) you'd rarely find me with any fish in the box—not because of current regulations, but because I hardly ever keep any fish. Now if you're going to gut-hook small fish on light tackle and 'play' them for fifteen minutes so you can get a good video for the friends and neighbors as you hold the poor devil up under the gill covers, please understand that you had better toss that one on the barbie when you get home—because its chances of survival are ZERO. My style is very different. I'm not looking to impress anyone. If I'm bait fishing, I use barbless circle hooks on my fifty pound test tackle. When a fish hits, the circle hook grabs him in the corner of his mouth—every time. I crank in thirty pound fish so fast that they don't even know what hit them. I never gaff a fish. I never even net a fish. I never lift a fish out of the water if I can help it unless there's a very specific or very special reason to do so. I try to avoid touching the fish at all and always unhook him in the water whenever possible. My bass rarely lose a single scale, never bleed a lot, and never lose any of their critical coating of slime. They're off to where they came from within three minutes of being hooked, and I am absolutely confident that although they may be a little confused by the experience, they're none the worse for wear.

When a fish I land is extraordinary, I keep it, and I do so without any sense of guilt because for every fish I keep I release over a hundred to fight another day. That's a lot more than can be said for the more 'sporting' guy who hooks a twenty pounder just short of his anal fin, plays the fish to death and hoists it high and dry for a digital shapshot before releasing it belly up. All of the shots you see in this book that seem to contradict what I've just said, really don't. They all either fit my current formula for keeping fish, or were caught before I adopted it. At any rate, added together they represent only the tiniest percentage of the fish I've caught over the years.

In addition, my research has convinced me that the very biggest females are not the most prolific members of the species and may, in fact, be in the least productive stage of their lives. Today, through my respect for marine biology I like to think that I have evolved into a true advocate of the striped bass, and I have little patience for those who mistreat these great fish without even realizing the damage they are actually doing."

BACK IN THE seventies, long before Billy had acquired the moniker of *The Greek,* he had been regularly clam-chumming boat-loads of medium sized stripers on a daily basis in the *Atlantic Beach* area. On the way in he'd stop by a commercial dock where he would get paid a pretty handsome sum for several hundred pounds of *market* fish each trip. Before returning to his slip in Oceanside, Billy would thoroughly clean up the old *Thompson* so there would be no telltale signs of bass for prying eyes to see. On almost every afternoon while tying up the boat Billy would return the greeting of an older man who regularly observed the young kid get back to the dock, rods in clear view, but always "fishless." One early evening after a particularly successful day which brought in almost two thousand dollars for

Billy, the old guy approached the youthful fisherman.

"Hey kid, I see you go out every day and never get nothing."

He handed him a plastic bag heavily packed with fluke fil-
lets. "It can be a little tricky catching fish these days. Take
them home to your mother and tell her you did good today."
Billy was stunned, so all he could say was "Gee, thank you."

Regardless of the species, resources have to be preserved.
Billy's methods demonstrate a real understanding of conservation and a true respect for the striped bass.

Sometimes things are not always what they appear to be.

Dark Nights ... Big Fish

I N EVERY FISHING SEMINAR I've ever spoken at I always start off by saying the same thing:

I teach the habits of striped bass, not just how to catch them.

I know that I run the risk of starting to sound like a broken record but I don't know any better way of making my point. I'm not going to send you to some hundred square foot box of water that may be loaded with stripers, but I am going to try to show you some universal methods to help you identify those areas for yourself, no matter where you fish.

In my youth I measured my own success by the size and numbers of bass that I caught. I fished mainly for the money, for the respect of the guys who I wanted respect from, and for the glory that came from catching monster-sized bass. Pretty much in that order. I won't say that I don't have an ego any more, but I will say that today my priorities have changed. Regardless of what you may have heard elsewhere, there are still plenty of very big striped bass around. I am convinced that there are survivors of some of the most successful year-classes of the sixties still lurking in the shadows of bridges during the very late fall of certain seasons. I know this because I have seen them with my own eyes. I have landed fish of nearly sixty pounds that were the midgets of pods of bass that included monsters whose size would be almost frightening to estimate. And I will never forget the fresh-caught ninety-one pounder curled in the fish box at Frank's *in the days of my youth. And we have all heard stories of the hundred pound-plus fish that have found their way into the commercial markets. You might find it hard to believe, but these are not just the legendary fish of bygone eras, they are fish that swim today. Not in any real numbers, of course. They were never around in any real numbers. But they are around—and they are the fish that define and dictate my priorities today. It is my search for these fish that has exposed me to such huge numbers of less impressive fish and has forced me to acquire the comprehensive knowledge that is required to encounter big striped bass with what some folks have described as startling consistency.*

Please don't get me wrong—I love to catch all sizes of striped bass—but it is only the pursuit and the promise of true monsters that keeps me living the life of a man who really needs to get a life.

But you don't have to mimic my existence to catch fish most of the time. You just have to pay more careful attention to what striped bass are interested in. Like any other wild animal, their number one priority is food. Because they are strong and resourceful animals they have more avenues to food than, say, the flounder—or the mossbunker.

All fish are opportunistic feeders and stripers will eat a segment of worm, just like a flounder, if that food source should find its way directly in front of a striper's nose. But the bass also has the ability and power to chase a mullet into the pounding surf of an ocean beach in the middle of a howling northeast storm that sweeps the current over the bottom faster than a four by four could keep pace in the sand. Or she could wait, totally motionless, in the shadowline of a bridge, for a lafayette to drift helplessly into her feeding zone.

Tide and current play the key role in this perennial feeding ritual because they dictate the movement and susceptibility of the striper's prey. In the back bays, outgoing tide washes bait out of shallow drains into adjacent deeper waters where bass lie in wait. Strong tides are the striped bass fisherman's greatest ally because they render the bass's forage far more vulnerable. This is true for any venue—bay, surf, open-ocean or at the bridges. When baitfish have to struggle against the power of a surging tide, their evasive capabilities are significantly diminished—and lunchtime for roccus *becomes far less stressful.*

Tide and **Current**. *The operation of these factors is so basic, so fundamental to success, that they have to become second nature to any striped bass fisherman.*

In striped bass fishing the full moon has long been considered the magic ingredient. Whenever I ask a fisherman to identify the one factor that has more influence on potential success with bass than any other, I almost always get a reference to the fish-producing reputation of the full moon. Sometimes I feel as though I'm asking the question of a community of werewolves in Transylvania, the intensity is so great.

I agree that the full moon is significant. It is a major factor because of what I've already explained about tide and current. The presence of the full moon generally equates to increased striped bass activity because it equates to stronger tidal activity. This is an astronomical fact that has been known throughout much of history. If bait fish are more susceptible to attack in strong tidal conditions, they become most vulnerable to predation in the strongest tides that accompany the periods of the full moon. But the full moon is a mixed blessing for many striped bass fishermen. This traditionally-perceived 'ultimate' fishing period can actually kill a bay bite entirely. The water moves harder, disorienting the bait fish as a positive consequence, but also floods the marshes with higher tides, pulling off large quantities of weed and debris and silting up the bay. The muddy, weed-choked waters that result often destroy the bite by making effective presentations impossible.

On the open waters of the ocean, on the other hand, an entirely different scenario holds true. 'Outside,' weed and silt are far less of a negative factor and the intensity of moonlight penetrating the depths actually helps to negate the effects of phosphorescence (fire in the water) that can otherwise destroy night-time ocean fishing efforts. The brightness of the moon actually reduces the contrast between the brightly glowing sub-surface plankton and what is normally their very dark watery backdrop. That is why a full moon is almost always a great ocean moon—and why its presence is so eagerly anticipated by striper fishermen who fish the outside. Just check the charter and party boat ads at Montauk or any other famous striper port. The biggest catches (but not necessarily the biggest fish) are generally reported on periods of the brightest moon.

A full moon at the surf line represents yet another range of possibilities and its influence can go either way. The increased tidal pull brings with it the distinct advantages of faster moving water, but excess weed and powerful tidal sweep often accompany the moon and can make for challenging conditions, at best—impossible conditions, at worst. Still, there is no doubt that the magical aura of the full moon remains a major draw for most surfcasters. Sometimes I think it's because the fishermen are mesmerized more by the dramatic interplay of the elements than the fish. A brisk fall night on a deserted beach with the moonbeams dancing off the whiteness of the curling surf—how romantic! And if you're lucky, you'll be able to fish effectively. And if you are, you could have the best night of your entire season.

But if there is truly a magical period to fish for big striped bass, the real magic will be found when that nearest of our celestial neighbors is totally dark—the period when the moon is new. *Throughout my thirty-four year obsession with striped bass I have never caught big fish with greater consistency than during the new phase of the moon, especially when fishing on the 'inside.' I believe that the period of the new moon actually multiplies the beneficial effects of the full moon but does so, for some reason that still eludes me, without the negative conditions so often produced by its brighter brother. The vast majority of my biggest stripers— fish going from over fifty—to well over sixty pounds have been caught on the dark side of the moon. The new moon has given me the best single night of my entire fishing career—four fish over fifty pounds, all caught within fifteen minutes of each other. There have been numerous other non-moon periods when I have caught many more big fish—bass ranging from thirty to forty pounds—but there has never been a time when I have landed more truly enormous fish in one outing. And one more thing. These fish have all been what I have been affectionately referring to as "late cruisers"—the last independent monsters that hang around for a* *week or two (sometimes three) after the crowds have left. I mean the fish crowds and the fishermen. These big stripers do what the largest members all migratory species do—they wait to gorge themselves before beginning their long journey (in this case) south. They hang out near the inlets and at the bridges. If pods of nice fat herring are going to be curious enough to investigate the strange beams of light penetrating the blackness of the rushing tide, why should these savvy monsters pass up the opportunity to revel in a last few very satisfying, very easy meals?*

And guess what? They never do.

"WHICH REMINDS ME of one of the more interesting outings of my career.

Another real late November, real late at night, or more accurately, real early in the morning. Whatever you would call three a.m.

So here I am on another new moon, this time at the *Swift Creek Bridge*, long after every guy with even a shred of sanity still left has hung it up for the season. The old decade would soon be on its way out and the tide was on its way in—not my choice for the direction of water movement—but something striking caught my eye, something I almost couldn't believe. Three huge fish were lined up in the shadowline, side by side. They all looked similar in length, but the middle fish was definitely a little longer and was clearly much wider than its tide-mates. I estimated the size of the outer fish to be in the mid-forties, and the middle fish to be something over fifty pounds.

I was all by myself, and my heart, which never beats very hard, was starting to pound.

My target was the fat middle fish. I surprised even myself with the perfect placement of the three-ounce, porkrind-tipped bucktail. I was right to be pleased, because it wasn't a second before the lure arched to within a foot of the monster's nose. Then, the clincher. Her pectoral fins began to quiver and I knew that she was committed to the strike. And she was— but so was the more impetuous fish to her immediate right who darted out and intercepted my offering a millisecond

"This wasn't the big fish. I definitely missed the big fish. Billy was probably casting to a **70** pound fish that night—or better!"

before it would have been inhaled by my target of choice. The hooked bass exploded downtide, under the bridge, assisted by a smoking new moon tide. I had to hang on for dear life and was amazed by how hard a time she was giving me for a fish that I considered to be only a mid-forty pounder. I finally landed this fish that was obviously much larger than I first thought. This fish had to be way over fifty. The other two fish were no longer anywhere to be seen.

This 'smaller' fish went into the back of my van and I made friends with a cup of coffee before my curiosity got the best of me. I don't carry a scale because I have never missed estimating the weight of a big fish by more than a pound. This fish looked much larger to me than I had originally thought so I witheld my personal estimate, thinking that my judgement might be clouded by cold and fatigue. With the sun coming up, I headed for a local bait and tackle shop. *Skip* was just unlocking the front door.

Certified scale, certified weight: fifty-nine pounds, even.

You have to understand. This wasn't the big fish. I definitely missed the big fish.

Whenever the opportunity arises, try giving a new moon in November a try. It doesn't always work, but when it does, believe me, it really does."

Flip The Calendar Page

W E'RE NOW IN REAL TIME, which is to say the very early spring, early in the new millenium. Reports of fish are spotty at best and the fanatics have been occupying their time with fishing shows and flea markets. Billy has been invited to speak at a local *CCA Seminar* along with some of the more highly visible personalities on the scene. He has been promoted as "one of the best 'big fish' surfcasters on the beach today," a description with which *The Greek* himself would have absolutely no argument.

I am looking forward to observing the public persona of my colorful *amigo*. Public speaking has never been very high on Billy's list of priorities (even though he has been much sought after to present the secrets of his success) and I have never actually heard him address a group on the subject of his fanaticism, or on any other subject for that matter. So this promises to be a very interesting event.

Basically, the room is filled with striped bass fishermen. Their levels of expertise are varied but not their levels of interest or enthusiasm. They all want to learn secrets of how to become better striped bass fishermen, just as they all want to do whatever they can, politically or otherwise, to see the species flourish. Lest anyone get the wrong impression, the two interests are far from being mutually exclusive. These guys are all willing to go the distance to insure not just the survival, but the proliferation of their beloved striped bass.

The exhibits are interesting and the speakers are informative, but I'm anxious to hear Billy's presentation. Really, that's why I came—and from the circle of admirers hovering around the striped bass photo-strewn table that Billy has set up, it seems that I'm not the only one with that interest. I sense that we are outside of *The Greek's* comfort zone, though, because the signature white painter's pants and insulated vest are conspicuously absent, swapped this day for more conventional jeans and shirt and a head of neatly combed hair that for once doesn't remind me of Svengali battling his way home in a strong nor'easter.

I'm not really surprised that for the most part Billy ignores the presentations of the other speakers. Neither I guess should I be surprised that he never uses any kind of notes or appears to spend any time at all in preparation. When the time comes, he just walks to the mic and announces,

"I'm *Billy the Greek*, and I'm going to tell you guys how to catch really big striped bass."

From that point on *The Greek* seems to go into autopilot. It's not that he delivers a canned speech on the techniques of striped bass fishing, it's that he is so immersed in his subject that the information just flows and flows. Billy pretty much speaks until he's told that he's out of time, because he will never have to cut things short because he's out of information—or because the group is drifting off into dream-land.

At first I thought that the audience would be satisfied with nothing less than GPS coordinates, or ranges, or exact tide/wind/bait/lure combinations—like the winning numbers to *Take Five*—but that was not the case. Instead of marking the hot-spots with a big "X" and sending participants on their way—they get straightforward fundamentals with detailed explanations of the reasons why things happen the way they do in the world of striped bass fishing.

The tide creates the bite. There will always be a prefer-ence stage—and you have to learn when it is.
Bait patterns denote the size of the fish that swim in an area—and the number of fish that will hang around. If there is no dense bait pattern, there will be very few fish or no fish at all.
The wind directs the placement of where the fish will eventually show up and the direction in which they will even-tually move...

It was the classic application of the "Give a man a fish/Teach a man to fish" parable.

In the early days of my career I spent twenty-six years in front of a classroom, disseminating information. Little did I know that Billy and I would end up sharing one of the strongest of common denominators. In the final analysis, we both were teachers, after all.

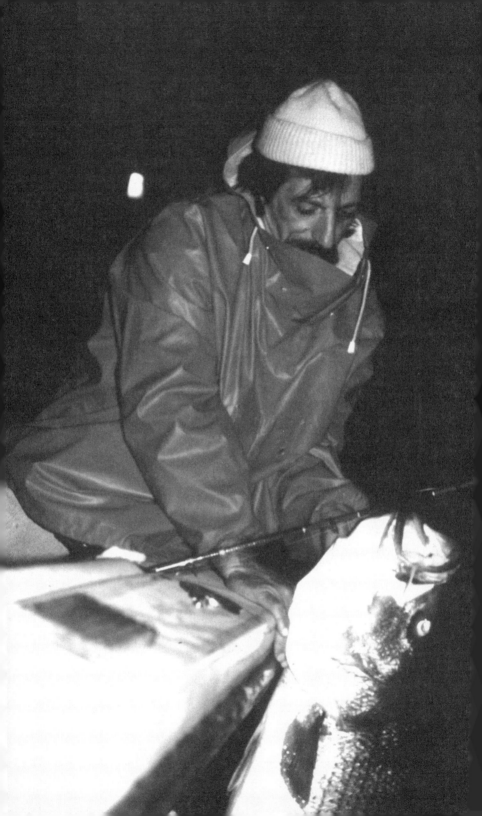

Hard-Core

*B*Y NOW YOU'VE FIGURED OUT *that the most deadly method for fooling giant stripers is by fishing with live or fresh bait. I've caught tons (and I really mean tons, literally) of big fish on artificials of every kind and I still do. But when it comes to developing consistency with these fish you've got to start learning bait and bait patterns. Most guys, when I ask them about natural baits, talk about bunker and live eels. Do you really believe that stripers live primarily on such a limited menu? Give me a break. If you haven't either figured out or haven't accepted that stripers, like any other predator, are opportunistic feeders you will never become much of a bass fisherman, plain and simple. If you think that a big bass does a lot of bait chasing, you will never be much of a big bass fisherman. Plain and simple. The fact is that certain bait will predominate in certain places at certain times of the year. It may very well be that the bottom is paved with an entirely different forage species than what you have been fruitlessly presenting as your offering. What might the big boys be stuffing themselves with locally? To mention only a few: calico crabs (big bass devour them like kids stuffing themselves with popcorn at a movie theatre); baby flounder and fluke—and not-so-baby flounder and fluke (I know a lot* *of party boat captains who equate the lack of flounder in the bay to the huge numbers of hungry springtime bass in the bay, and I fully concur); baby blowfish (think of them as dumplings to stripers); porgies (bass have good taste); blackfish (everyone knows that, right?); weakfish, digger crabs—and more exotic, but often very abundant species like manta shrimp, lafayettes and lizard fish. And yes, big stripers do consume tons of eels, bunker, mackerel, herring and mullet. Trust me, though, even this list is far from complete.*

"'How do I know these things,' you ask? Well, how much of a forensic marine biologist are **you**? I've had to become a master at identifying the partially digested remains of virtually every element of the striper's diet. This doesn't mean that you must always "match the hatch" in order to catch big bass (sometimes it's both illegal and unethical to do so) but it does mean that you must learn to read the bait patterns so you can gain the upper hand. The presence of baby flounder in a big striper's stomach doesn't mean that you have to use undersized flounder, illegally, for bait—but it does give you an invaluable piece of information—which is that these fish have been feeding on or near a mud bottom. Calico crabs tell you that the feeding zone has been on or near sandy bottoms. And how much does it take to figure out that if you're hitting fish on a mussel bottom and you lose them, that if you can set up on another mussel bottom, downtide and with similar tidal conditions, you can probably get them going again? It's not, as everyone likes to say these days, 'rocket science,' but it is definitely a form of science and it takes a lot of time and effort to learn. But if you learn it well, very few guys will be able to keep up with you."

Maybe now you can understand why the sharpies aren't going to be so quick to give away the keys to the kingdom.

I'VE NEVER PERSONALLY been one for making the best of circumstances. I far prefer for the circumstances to be advantageous and then at least I have a chance of producing at my best. But in the world of fishing there are far too many variables over which I have absolutely no control and that is why, I suspect, my successes are so few and far between.

I love offshore fishing for anything from blues to tuna— but I've also been known to defeat the palliative effect of every motion sickness treatment known to man. No longer deluded by the naiveté of youth, you might understand why my blue-water trips have become extremely infrequent. That leaves the bay, for the most part, including all types of bottom fishing. But I hate fishing with a lot of lead when the tide is too intense. Or when the wind is blowing much stronger than a gentle breeze. Or when the chill pierces through you before the first fish has even sniffed your bait. Now I don't want to come off as a total wimp, but I really do prefer conditions to be what I would describe as favorable.

I fully recognize that there is, as in any other pursuit, a range of commitment to the sport of fishing. On a graph running left to right, *pansy* to *fanatic*, I suppose I'd be near the left-hand border. I know that many striper fishermen would definitely be crowding the right edge of the chart. And Billy would be somewhere off the radar screen.

That's one of the points that *The Greek* so emphatically makes whenever he shares his method with disciples. If you're going to enjoy a measure of success in this game, you have to squeeze the max out of every opportunity. Which means you have to be willing to fish hard under any set of conditions, even if that means sacrifice and physical discomfort.

"When I fish in tournaments, I hear a lot of guys bitch about bad conditions. Bad tides, the wrong wind, too much weed—you name it. They like to come up with excuses for not doing well. I don't buy it. Back in my rabid pool-playing days, one of the greatest masters of the game, *Willie Mosconi,* gave me the kind of advice that stays with you all your life. It had to do with playing conditions at a particular tournament where things weren't what they should have been. Most of the players were pissed that they couldn't get together their best stuff. But Willie pointed out that when the lighting is bad, it's bad for everyone. When the table is bad, it's bad for everyone. When conditions are bad, they're bad for everyone. So you should let the bad conditions work to your advantage by establishing a positive attitude when everyone else is screwing up their games even worse than they have to. That way, bad conditions will actually work to give you the edge.

He who adjusts first, wins.

All kinds of fisherman, newcomers and experts alike, ask me how I manage to catch so many big fish year in, year out. There really isn't any big mystery and I'm always willing to explain. I have been fishing for bass most of my life. I fish every day during the season, morning and night—and many days outside of the season just to expand my base of knowledge. I do not let work interfere with fishing. I conduct my business affairs intensely, but I conduct them around my commitment to stripers. I fish under virtually any conditions. But most importantly, I never fail to adjust to the methods that are needed to catch big fish. Sometimes these required adjustments are major in proportion, but more often than not they're subtle wiggles that make the difference between big scores and striking out.

If I had a few bucks for every time I've seen guys fishing the wrong live bait I could probably retire on the interest from investing in that bonanza. Like drifting live eels during the day in the back when the fish are demolishing peanut bunker on top. Or trolling outside with bunker spoons in forty feet of water when monsters are feasting on baby kingfish just outside the surf line. What about when all the reports state that the action is on the first of the outgoing (and it is true that tons of small fish **may be** biting on that tide) but the really big fish are feeding on the last of the incoming?

Which reminds me of the questions I get regarding published fishing reports. Guys will always tell me how they know that these reports are useless bullshit because they feel that they're old and outdated before they even hit the presses. I tell them that the fact is these reports can be extremely useful if you understand that bass are what I call 'directional' fish that travel north in the spring and south in the fall. The fishing reports present very useful information on the size of fish, the immediate areas that they're in and the bait patterns that they're on—which can orient you pretty well **if** you have the ability to extrapolate the movement of fish based upon a solid understanding of the habits of big stripers. But too many guys blindly chase the fishing reports, especially the news of a big solitary fish, which will almost always put them in position a day late and a dollar short. If you don't believe me, just ask any equities day trader who thinks he can hit it big chasing a major price jump in a penny stock. You've got to learn how to read the trends. Followers are usually left to pick up the scraps. *Learn to adjust. Modify. Adapt. Catch fish.*"

"In the late 90's I was on a consistent bite of big fish at *Tobay*. After two days I called in a couple of close fishing buddies to get in on the action. It's pretty hard to keep quality fishing like this under wraps during the day but it's not very difficult, after the sun goes down, to remain on your own. You wouldn't think so, though, because the beach is just so big. But it never ceases to amaze me how most 'fishermen' will plant themselves at the scene of the last reported action and forget the fact that most fish actually **swim** along the beach. For real, they actually swim. We followed the movement of these fish west and caught them almost non-stop on bunker chunks for four nights running.

The bulk of casters thought the bite was over. No, all you needed to do was to adjust."

"By now you know that I'm kind of serious about what I do. But that doesn't mean I lack a sense of humor.

One day I'm at *West Gilgo* with *John P* and *Johnny K*. The fish are way off the beach so I'm hitting them with my famous bullet casts—while these guys are striking out for lack of power."

Billy's eleven and a half foot "giant-killer" was launching his casts nearly into lunar orbit when he decided to really push the envelope. A bit too far, I'm sorry to say, for on the very next cast the air was punctuated with the unmistakable whip-crack report of snapping graphite. Silence reigned for an ensuing instant as Billy's disciples attempted to stifle their reaction, fearing the wrath of *The Greek* which has been known to lead to expulsion from the *Garden of Giant Stripers*. But Billy was actually the first to totally crack up, four hundred dollar custom rod notwithstanding. When the laughter finally quieted down *Johnny K* offered Billy his spare *Luxor* spinning outfit to get back in on the action. Not surprisingly, Billy declined.

"The rod had snapped off just ahead of the reel seat. I broke the end off as cleanly as I could, hacked off the first guide and wrapped my *Squidder* on with electrical tape. Then I proceeded to catch a thirty-pounder on my first cast. Both Johns just shook their heads. I kept fishing.

I named that rod *'Stubby.'* Not quite up to my standards anymore, but it still catches fish.

Like I said, I never forgot the words I heard from the master many years ago—*He who adjusts first wins.*"

I've always believed that absence really does make the heart grow fonder. So I've always thought that if I ever got to the point where I could catch big striped bass with any real consistency, the thrill would eventually diminish. Through my association with Billy though, I've come to realize that such would probably never be the case. Not that I'd ever be any good at catching bass myself—but that I've come to understand why the fascination with this fish never seems to end. Much of it has to do with what has always lured us to the sea—the beauty, the serenity, the mystery. But a more significant part of the game, for men like Billy, has to do with the endless challenge. Not just the specific challenge of tracking down a record striped bass, but the challenge of the entire experience.

As much as Billy knows about the striper's ways and the striper's domain, he is the first to admit that there is much more that remains unknown. All of the impressive marine technology that we have access to today can only take us so far. All of the accumulated knowledge that fishermen have gathered prior to the electronics revolution can only do the same. Then there is the question of unshared knowledge, the secrets that have gone to the grave with the passing of the striper-fishing legends. And the question of technique and method that can't be taught, even if there were a desire to pass the knowledge on—a subtle motion of the hand, a pause so slight in a retrieve that even its practitioner is unaware that he is making it. Add a sea that is forever changing and its creatures that must forever adapt—both to nature's twists and turns as well as to the challenges wrought by man.

So mysteries remain—and persist so tenaciously as to render the pursuit of striped bass **the** perennial challenge. That is why it's hard to become bored with the hunt for these fish, especially the wise old monsters that Billy targets every time he goes out.

"You have to understand that I'm not like most guys who would be thrilled just to catch a keeper or two on most trips out. I really don't want to sound arrogant, but if you haven't figured out by now that I'm not fishing for ordinary striped bass when I go out, then you haven't been paying much attention. Every single time I leave the dock or hit the beach I truly believe that I'm going to catch fish that are up to my standards. Come on, you should know what I mean. Big fish—forty pounds and over. No, I'm not a total idiot—I know that there will be times when fish like this won't be around—but if I just went by the reports that circulate, I'd never get a decent bass. And I've never had a season when I don't get at least fifty fish over thirty pounds. Never. Not in the past thirty years.

Do you know how many times I read that all the fish being caught are in the 'teens,' or 'low twenties'—and then go out and catch *thirties* and *forties*? Or that there are no big fish around any more—none—and I land a fifty before the ink is dry on the reports. I'm not saying that you can manufacture fish when there aren't any, but I am saying that when the big fish stop committing suicide there will still be big fish around, but they're going to be smarter and more selective and you're going to have to work harder to get them. And guess what? As the fish get harder and harder to find, most guys start losing interest. That's actually a plus for guys like me. Have you ever been on a party boat when the fishing is slow and most of the fares start laying back, drinking beers and waiting for someone else to demonstrate that there are still signs of life in the water? The slower it gets the more 'fishermen' start dropping out. Then some kid hooks the biggest fish of the day and all hell breaks loose. Everyone's back in the water and hot to get the next one—now that someone else has demonstrated that the fish may actually be there. When the going gets tough...

A while back I was speaking at a seminar. I guess I should be more careful about what I say sometimes, but there's not much chance of that happening. Anyway, I was scheduled to talk on 'targeting big striped bass.' One of the first things I said was that when I'm at a spot where all of the fish I'm catching are small—teens and low-twenties—I leave that spot and head elsewhere. Some guys think I'm full of shit when I say things like that, but anyone who knows me knows that I mean it very simply and very sincerely. You just aren't going to catch big fish in an area that's holding nothing but a ton of schoolies. I'm not looking for keepers. I'm not fishing for the market. I want monsters because I know there are still monsters out there. That's why I'm never bored. How could I be? True, I don't exactly tremble with excitement every time I slide another twenty-five pounder back in the water. But how do you think I feel when I observe, as clearly as a log suspended in the water, a sixty inch fish finning just below the surface in the shadowline? Trust me, it's not hallucination. Not my vivid imagination. And I'm not talking about a once in a lifetime observation. I'm talking maybe half a dozen times. Sixty inch—sometimes even bigger fish that dwarf the current world's record. Just waiting for the guy who can figure out how to catch them.

No, I don't think that I'll ever get tired of this game. Not in this lifetime, anyway."

That opportunity was to present itself yet again toward the close of the last decade, just as the year slipped into winter.

The calendar of official seasons never meant much to Billy and it has always been his custom to check things out before accepting that it was really over for another year. He did this for three reasons. First, he found that these late observations always added something to his body of knowledge. Second, it was almost guaranteed that he would be alone. And third, the largest striped bass he has ever encountered have been at the periphery of the season's end.

In most years, instinct pulled all bass south on cue and by late November they were nothing but a memory. Even the biggest, solitary *late-cruisers* would be gone. But those odds never stopped *The Greek* from making his final rounds, sometimes even after the flakes began to fall. If the moon were new any time before mid-December, at least half a dozen outings were guaranteed. In this year the moon was new on the fourteenth of the month.

These trips always followed the same pattern. If any big stripers were still hanging around they would be there for one reason. Food. But they would not venture very far from the inlets, their avenue to the ocean's route south. Once again, the combination led to bridges. Once again, Billy would walk the spans, rod at the ready, but never casting blindly.

"This had been a good season for me with quite a few forties and one fish over fifty. I felt that the big one might still be hanging out, even though it was real late. I'm funny at the end of the year—I just don't want to give it up. I've seen and caught too many monsters at this time to say that it's over. But I had been walking both sides of four different bridges for five nights on both sides of the new moon without any signs of life—not even bait in the water. I started to feel that it was time to pronounce the patient dead. I never actually take any casts when I do this, I just scour the shadowline for very big, very dark silhouettes. And there weren't any. None.

I talked with Mike about what happened next, just before I headed for the warmth of my van for the last time that season. We both agreed that if anything sounded like it pushed the limits of credibility, what happened next did. We talked about leaving it out of the book for that reason. But it happened, so here it is.

I was three lightpoles from the southwestern corner of the bridge, still compelled by force of habit to remain focused on the water as I walked, expecting nothing.

Then, she rose to just below the surface.

What can I say? I have seen a thousand big fish in the shadowline at night. Over the years quite a few guys have been treated to similar observations. A lot more have been present when these fish have shown, but they have insisted that they've seen nothing. I can't help that. What I see, I see. Most of the time, what I see I also catch.

What I saw that night was spectacular, very quietly spectacular.

The fish rose from the bottom, gently tagged a surface

bubble, then settled down to a foot below the surface. Many times under these circumstances a fish appears as nothing more than a very dark, velvety shadow. That shadow almost always remains perfectly motionless. Companions who have been with me tell me that they can perceive the shadow but are unable to recognize any features of the fish at all. This night, I don't see how that failure of perception could have been possible. The water was black, but totally transparent. The size of this fish made it appear as though I was viewing it through the zoom lens of a camera. Anyone could have perceived what he was looking at. And they would have been stunned if they knew anything about striped bass—because they were observing a world's record fish. In a way I was sorry that no one would be able to corroborate what was there to be seen, yet I was really glad that I was alone. I had felt for many years that this was the way I wanted it to be. Me and the great fish. Pretty corny, eh? But here we were.

I was prepared. I was always prepared at this time of year. My equipment was in perfect condition. The fish was obviously there to eat—and just might be about to make the first very serious mistake of her life. I had been through this drill many times before and knew what had to be done. I couldn't help but recall the monster that had made her appearance in virtually the same location several years previously. That memory carried with it the frustration of failure. But this was a different time and a different opportunity—even though I considered the possibility that this could be the very same fish. It could actually be the same fish, only bigger—and wiser.

I knew what I had done wrong then. At least I knew what I had done before—that didn't work anyway. The biggest problem in a situation like this is the shallowness of experience. I believe that I have witnessed more of these extraordinary striped bass than anyone, yet the sum total of my knowledge is still limited to no more than a half-dozen such encounters. Still, I never panic. But I've been there enough times to realize that what works with other big fish probably won't work with these fish. That much I know because I've tried my best moves before and have come up short ninety percent of the time. And I have never succeeded in hooking a fish quite like the one below me, calmly finning in the moving tide. So that you know what I'm talking about here, let me remind you that I have weighed in a sixty-four pound eleven ounce fish. That's a magnificent striped bass, but I'm talking much, much bigger here. In most cases, as on this night, there is only a single fish present, but it's a fish that has been around a very long time and has probably seen everything there is to see. There was never really a mystery as to why big striped bass attack a lure or strike a bait. But with fish like these, I can't be sure that all the standard rules don't have to be called off. Still, this particular member of the elite clan of monsters would see my bucktail, painstakingly customized to replicate the herring that I knew she must be there to eat—presented in a way that I was convinced would provoke a strike. Presented in a way that was different than what had been tried—and failed—before."

It didn't happen very often, but on this last trip of the season, on this freezing December night, my chance had come again.

Epilogue

A S WE GO TO PRESS IN THE LATE SPRING of 2002 Billy is waiting for the delivery of a new motor for his boat. Not that there was anything wrong with the old Mercury that has served him so well over the past seven years—just that he doesn't want to chance even the possibility of a problem during the height of the rapidly approaching season. He's not very happy though, because there's been a delay in shipment and things are not quite where he'd want them to be.

The wind hasn't stopped blowing hard for two weeks. On my customary trips down *Wantagh Parkway* to *Field Six* the flags have been whipping out flat in the fresh breeze—off the ocean and west mostly, but on occasion from every other quadrant of the compass. The gulls are always there. The sea never rests.

Reports of striped bass are everywhere from the Hudson to the south shore bays. The winter has been mild and the fish are here early. Or perhaps they never left. Walking along the *Jones Beach* fishing piers with my wife the other day a particularly fixated gull caught my eye. I traced the angle of his

focus to a small striped bass just dead and rolling in the gentle waves generated by a passing boat. The fish was a short and had probably been released with the best of intentions that turned out to be not good enough. Sad, I felt. But this young bass made me think about Billy's attitude toward releasing fish and I knew that he was right about his method. The gull never quit its gaze, convinced that there had to be a way to somehow capitalize on this serendipitous gift of nature.

After all these years it's still hard for me to say why Billy does what he does. It's too easy to say only that it's the challenge, even though I've made that statement in the past. At the very least I'd have to add that it's the mystery as well. And the beauty. And the isolation. And the independence. And more.

The amazing thing about seeking out the definitive is that there really isn't any such thing. And when records are broken there is no guarantee that they will be broken by those who have labored the hardest or the longest. Or by those who are most deserving. Yet I feel in my heart, after all these years, that *The Greek* will eventually capture the largest striped bass on record during his lifetime. Only I'm not so sure that anyone will ever know that he did. Not because Billy was ever a modest guy, but because when you've become the predator, it's hard to see your brother beaten.

We'll have to wait and see. But if fishing legends actually do exist, that just might be the type of stuff that defines what they're really made of.

About The Author

IN NOVEMBER OF 2000 MICHAEL CINQEMANI retired from a thirty-two-year career with the New York City Board of Education where he served in positions ranging from junior high school English teacher to Acting Community Superintendent of a 26,000 student school district in Queens, New York. Although most of his past writing efforts have been centered in the fields of English literature and secondary education, fishing has remained a lifelong interest and love.

Night Tides presents Mr. Cinqemani's first published venture into a world that has fascinated him since childhood. It has been his intention for many years to chronicle the true story of his longtime friend and sporadic fishing buddy, Billy *The Greek* Legakis.

Michael lives on Long Island and is married to Rosalie, his wife of thirty-four years. They have two adult children, Michael and Christopher.